THE CATHOLIC UNIVERSITY OF AMERICA
CANON LAW STUDIES
NUMBER 67

THE ADMINISTRATION OF SEMINARIES

HISTORICAL SYNOPSIS
AND
COMMENTARY

A DISSERTATION

Submitted to the Faculty of Canon Law of the Catholic University of America in Partial Fulfillment of the Requirements for the Degree of

DOCTOR OF CANON LAW

by

JOSEPH GODFREY COX, A.B., J.C.L.,
Priest of the Archdiocese of Philadelphia

THE CATHOLIC UNIVERSITY OF AMERICA
WASHINGTON, D. C.
1931

Nihil Obstat:

VALENTINUS T. SCHAAF, O.F.M., J.C.D.,

Censor Deputatus.

Washingtonii, D. C., die XX Aprilis, 1931.

Imprimatur:

✠ D. CARD. DOUGHERTY,

Archiepiscopus Philadelphiensis,

Philadelphiae, die XXI Aprilis, 1931.

"Nord-Amerika" Press, Philadelphia, Pa.

TABLE OF CONTENTS

PART II

PRESENT LEGISLATION

CHAPTER V

CHAPTER VI

CHAPTER VII

FOREWORD

Clerical education has always been considered a most important phase of ecclesiastical discipline. The concern of the Church for the proper training of her clergy has been reflected from the earliest ages of the Christian era in many legislative enactments. Yet prior to the sixteenth century no one type of institution had proved of such permanent stability and practical efficacy as to warrant its choice as the sole guardian of clerical education. The problem of clerical training was among the many that confronted the Council of Trent, and the solution offered by the Council was the institution of ecclesiastical seminaries. This was prompted not only by the manifest decadence in clerical education and the necessity for reform in clerical discipline in general, but also by the realization that the very character of the Christian Priesthood, its supreme importance in the spiritual fabric of Christianity, and the necessity for integrity in the daily ministry of the priest, all postulate a specialized training that can best be secured only in such an institution. The wisdom and permanent value of their action is evident from the fact that the Tridentine seminary still remains the pattern upon which all our seminaries are constructed, and that the provisions of the original decree of the Council have been incorporated substantially into the New Code of Canon Law.

The historical synopsis which constitutes the first part of this dissertation is necessarily only a brief general survey. The dissertation is intended primarily to be a commentary on the Code legislation, and this fact, together with a lack of many original sources, precludes a critical and comprehensive treatment of all the legislative developments in the history of clerical education. Moreover, the nature of the legislation on seminaries rendered it necessary to omit many important juridical developments which ordinarily would be treated in an historical introduction to Code legislation. Much of the latter, with reference to seminaries, is based entirely on the law of the Council of Trent, and decisions and decrees which interpreted the Tridentine decree also had to serve as interpretations of the canons in the Code. The commentary on the Code is restricted to those canons which treat of the internal administration of seminaries. For the sake of clarity and logical order, this phase of seminary administration has been viewed from the aspect of the rights and duties of the Bishop, the seminary officials, and the two advisory commissions instituted by the Council of Trent. The administration of temporalities and the requirements of the curriculum of studies are of so wide a canonical scope that each would require a separate dissertation for a fair and adequate exposition.

The writer desires to express his gratitude to the Faculty of Canon Law for their advice and encouragement. He is also greatly indebted to Rev. William Ferry, Rev. Mark Ebner, Rev. James Lauer, Rev. William Farrell and Rev. Robert White for their kindly and generous assistance in the preparation and publication of this dissertation.

CHAPTER ONE

Preliminary Discussion

1.—The right of the Church to the Exclusive Supervision of Clerical Education

The legislation of the Church on clerical education is based on the fundamental principle that, by virtue of her Divine institution and supernatural end, she is endowed with the inherent right and power to do whatever is deemed necessary for the salvation of souls.[1] The Catholic Church was instituted by Christ for a definite end and purpose, namely the sanctification of men, and therefore, she has the right to use those means that are morally necessary to attain it.[2] The message of salvation was entrusted to the Apostles and their successors in the Priesthood, and the education and training of the latter falls strictly within the competence of the Church. Experience has demonstrated that this training cannot be properly imparted in a secular institution. The Church, therefore, has not only a proper and exclusive right to supervise the education of those whose duty it will be to perform ecclesiastical functions, but as a corollary of this, the exclusive right to erect and to supervise seminaries for the training of her clergy.[3]

The Church is a supernatural society, perfect in its own order, and absolutely independent of the State.[4] The former, not the latter, has been charged with the sanctification of souls,[5] for the end of the State is to promote directly and immediately the temporal welfare of its subjects. The Church, through her Priesthood, aids the State to accomplish this by promoting religion, the foundation of morality, but this does not render clerical education directly an object of civil competence.[6] The Church would not be an absolutely independent

[1] Cavagnis, *Institutiones Juris Publici Ecclesiastici*, III, 39.

[2] Wernz, *Jus Decretalium*, III, n. 72; Cavagnis, *op. cit.*, p. 44.

[3] Cappello, *Summa Juris Publici*, pp. 515-16.

[4] Leo XIII, encycl. "*Immortale Dei*," Nov. 1, 1885—Fontes, n. 592, Epist. "*Jampridem*," Jan. 6, 1886—Fontes, n. 593; Pius IX, *Syllabus Errorum* (1864)—prop. 19, Fontes, n. 543.

[5] "Dux hominibus esse ad coelestia non civitas sed Ecclesia debet"—Leo XIII, encycl. "*Immortale Dei*," Nov. 1, 1885—Fontes, n. 592.

[6] Cavagnis, *op. cit.*, pp. 48-49.

society unless she possessed the unquestioned right to supervise clerical education. Any contrary contention seems absurd, for otherwise there would be the possibility of a heretical and inimical State endowed with divinely conferred power over the institution of the Christian Priesthood.[7] Moreover, the Church has maintained this right at all times, and in all circumstances.[8] The secular authority has often claimed some jurisdiction over clerical education,[9] but the Church has never, even in her concordats with various nations, made any concessions of her fundamental rights in this matter.[10] At the most, concessions of minor moment have been made, such as the use of the national tongue in teaching certain profane subjects.[11]

Some objection might be made to the foregoing assertions because of the prominent part played by some secular rulers, such as Charlemagne, in the history of clerical education. The legislation contained in certain imperial capitularies on clerical education is understandable when one considers that ecclesiastics were practically the sole custodians of learning up to the inception of the universities, and that clerics and lay students were trained in the same institutions.[12] The efforts of these rulers to promote and stabilize education had the cooperation, support, and approval of the ecclesiastical authorities.[13] Nor was there any derogation from ecclesiastical jurisdiction in the accord of the Church with the State regarding certain matters of external administration,[14] as in the submission of the annual fin-

[7] "Denique absonum plane est dicere Christum Dominum gravissimam hanc curam, non Ecclesiae sed Statui forte haereticae et Ecclesiae inimicissimo commississe aut saltem Ecclesiam hac in re statui subordinatae."—Wernz, *Jus Decretalium*, III, n. 93.

[8] Themistor, *L'Instruction et l'Education du clergé*, p. 36; Capello, *Summa Juris Publici*, p. 516; Wernz, *loc. cit.*

[9] Maitre, *Les Ecoles Episcopales et Monastiques*, pp. 122-23; Themistor, *op. cit.*, p. 103.

[10] Capello, *op. cit.*, p. 515; Concordat between Pius VII and Napoleon (1803)—Nussi, *Conventiones de Rebus Ecclesiasticis*, p. 144; Concordat between Pius VII and Maximilian of Bavaria (1817)—Nussi, *op. cit.*, p. 149; Concordat between Leo XII and the Swiss cantons—Nussi, *op. cit.*, p. 343; Concordat between Pius IX and Costa Rica (1853)—Nussi, *op. cit.*, p. 300; Concordat between Pius IX and the Republic of Gautemala (1852)—Mercati, *Raccolta di Concordati*, p. 816.

[11] Concordat between Holy See and Russia (1882)—Mercati, *op. cit.*, p. 1017; Concordat between Holy See and Island of Malta (1890)—Mercati, *op. cit.*, p. 1072.

[12] Rashdall, *Universities of Europe in the Middle Ages*, I, 33; Maitre, *op. cit.*, p. 118; Limmer, *Bildungszustande und Bildungseideen des XIII Jahrhunderts*, p. 83.

[13] "Carolus Magnus sua capitularia proposuit, non invita, sed consentiente et approbante Ecclesia"—Wernz, *Jus Decretalium*, III, n. 93.

[14] *Bachofen, Summa Juris Publici Ecclesiastici*, p. 90.

ancial reports of the seminaries of France to the *Bureau des Séminaires* established by Napoleon. The Bureau was not permitted to interfere in any way with the disciplinary direction of the seminaries.[15]

2.—The Right and Duty of the Bishop to Supervise Clerical Education

Our Divine Lord gave to the Apostles the mandate, "Going, therefore, teach ye all nations . . .", and this same obligation is incumbent upon their successors, the Bishops of the Catholic Church. The latter, taken collectively and as a college, teach with infallible authority; individually, however, their jurisdiction is restricted to the diocese over which they preside, in which, indeed, they teach with authority, by virtue of the mission which they hold from Jesus Christ, but not infalliblly.[16] The teaching function of the episcopate, inherent in their office, has been exercised since the earliest ages of the Christian era in the education of candidates for the clerical State.[17] This exercise represents a right which emerges as an inevitable corollary from the considerations in the preceding article. The independence of the Church with regard to clerical education, which has its origin in divine law, necessarily renders independent any institution intended for that purpose, and places its administration wholly within the scope of ecclesiastical competence. The proximate and immediate jurisdiction over such institutes is the function of individual Bishops, since they are vested with ordinary and supreme jurisdiction in their respective dioceses. The principle of episcopal independence in matters spiritual [18] has been vindicated with reference to seminaries in all the concordats previously mentioned.[19]

Pope Leo XIII[20] has given a brief, but comprehensive summary of the dogmatic arguments for the rights of Bishops in the matter of clerical education. The Church has the exclusive power to legislate on those things which pertain to her interior life, a right guaranteed by her Divine Founder. This power is exercised by individual Bishops in their dioceses. By its very nature, it embraces all things necessary for clerical discipline. Moreover, the command to teach

[15] A. J. P., XXII, 705.

[16] Tanquerey, *Synopsis Theologiae Dogmaticae*, I, 586.

[17] Lowrie, *The Church and its Organization*, p. 221; Marcault, *L'Education des Clercs*, p. 67; Badii, *Institutiones Juris Canonici*, II, 147.

[18] C. 6, X, I, tit. 33.

[19] Vide note 11.

[20] Epistle "*Jampridem*," Jan. 6, 1886—Fontes, n. 593.

all nations renders it incumbent on the members of the episcopate to impart religious truths to their subjects, and this certainly implies the necessity of securing integrity of life and doctrine in those who are to aid in the teaching office—namely, the priests who are to be the light of the world and the legates of Christ among His people. These arguments were deemed incontrovertible by the saintly Pontiff, and his conclusion is that ". . . none other than the Bishop has the right and duty of instructing those youths whom God, in His singular bounty, has taken from among men to be the dispensers of His mysteries." [21]

3.—*The Origin of the Term "Seminary." Its Use in Canon Law*

The Fathers of the Council of Trent used the word *seminary* to designate institutions for clerical training. The term is derived from the Latin word for "*seed*" (semen), and indicates primarily a plot of ground where seeds are grown, and from which they are afterwards transplanted,[22] although applied meanings are found even in classical Latin literature.[23] The term was applied in a general way to schools by Charles V, in an address before the Diet of Augsburg, in 1548.[24] The first evidence of its use in a strictly ecclesiastical document is found in the decree on the reformation of the Church in England, promulgated by Cardinal Pole in 1556.[25] It is there applied exclusively to an institution destined to train candidates for the Priesthood. Within a short time the word was applied generally to institutions where Catholic clerics were taught, and in 1678 it was defined as such in a current English dictionary.[26] In modern English the term is used indiscriminately with reference to all institutions, whether Catholic or Protestant, in which theological training is given.

Authors give substantially the same definition of the word "seminary" in its canonical significance. Two examples may be cited:

[21] "Nemini dubium esse potest non aliis quam episcopis jus munusque esse docendi et instituendi juvenes quos Deus singulari beneficio ex hominibus assumit, ut sint ministri ac dispensatores mysteriorum suorum. . . . Sit igitur integrum, sit liberum, jus et potestas, episcopis in seminariorum palaestrae mansuetae Christi militiae fingendae conferre operam."—Leo XIII, *ibidem*.

[22] *Harper's Latin Dictionary*, v. seminarium; Freund-Leverett, *Latin Lexicon*, v. seminarium.

[23] *New English Dictionary* (Murray, Craigie, Bradley), v. seminary.

[24] A. J. P., I, 667.

[25] Mansi, XXIII, 1029-30; A. J. P., I, 668.

[26] *New English Dictionary*, loc. cit.

1. "A seminary is an ecclesiastical college, established by competent authority, in which clerics are trained in letters and sacred sciences, and in all things necessary for the clerical state." [27]

2. "A seminary is a religious institute or college in which students for the secular priesthood are received, maintained, instructed, and trained in ecclesiastical science and discipline, according to the norms enacted by the Council of Trent." [28]

The first definition embraces a wider scope, and includes all institutions where students for the Priesthood are trained, including those of the various religious orders. The second definition restricts the term to seminaries established according to the Tridentine decree, which mentions only diocesan and provincial seminaries, although other types have appeared in the interval between the Council of Trent and the promulgation of the Code. The fundamental difference between the various kinds of seminaries usually arises either from territorial limitations or from the scope of their respective curricula. Under the first distinction may be mentioned:

1. *Diocesan* seminaries: established in a diocese for the education of the clerical students of that diocese.

2. *Provincial* seminaries: established for all the students intended for the various dioceses comprising a province.

3. *Regional* or *Interdiocesan* seminaries: instituted by several dioceses in a region for their students, though not necessarily of the same province.

4. *National* seminaries: erected for the students of some particular nationality, usually at Rome.

5. *Universal* seminaries: intended for students from the entire world.

While there is a practical difference between provincial and interdiocesan seminaries, they are equivalent in law.[29] Seminaries of religious orders are called by the code "*Domus Studiorum.*" [30]

The further classification on the basis of curricular differences comprises the following:

1. *Major* seminaries: in which students who have completed a course in humanities are prepared for the reception of sacred orders by the study of philosophy and theology.

---

[27] Badii, *Institutiones Juris Canonici*, II, 146.
[28] Wernz, *Jus Decretalium*, III, n. 91; Michelctti, *De Regimine*, p. 34.
[29] Augustine, *Commentary on Canon Law*, VI, 379; Canon 1357 §4.
[30] C. 587 §2.

2. *Minor* seminaries: in which profane letters and sciences are studied as a basis for higher studies in philosophy and theology.

These are the usual classes of seminaries mentioned by authors.[31] Besides these, there are the so-called "*mixed*" seminaries, or combined colleges and seminaries, attended by both students for the clerical state and lay students, even though the latter have no intention of entering the Priesthood.[32] A seminary erected by the authority of the Holy See, or to which its supervision is reserved, is called a "*pontifical*" seminary. All regional seminaries come under the latter classification.[33]

4.—*The Necessity and Utility of Seminaries*

The necessity of a long period of training for the candidate for the clerical state is evident. If it were only a question of knowing the fundamentals of faith and of administering the Sacraments, a few months would suffice. Far more than this is required. The clerical student must make a thorough and exhaustive study of the dogmatic tenets of the Catholic faith, in order that he may be able to defend its doctrines against argumentative attacks by those outside the Church; and that he may be capable of imparting a more comprehensive knowledge of them to the faithful within the Church. The latter is more requisite than ever in this age of Catholic action and the lay apostolate. The priest must know the moral teachings of the Church, for otherwise he will not be able to advise the faithful in their problems, administer to their spiritual ills, or expound to them the principles that must govern their daily lives. And finally, the priest must be familiar with the liturgy of the Church and the rubrics which govern it. In addition to this essential religious knowledge, the priest, as the leader of his people and the representative of the Church, must also possess a certain general culture which is the inheritance of educated men.

History has proved that the training of clerics cannot be accomplished properly in secular institutions. Reason itself necessitates the same conclusion, when one considers not only the highly specialized knowledge that is required, but also the very dignity of the

[31] Wernz, *Jus Decretalium*, III, n. 91; Micheletti, *De Regimine*, pp. 34-38; Bargilliat, *Praelectiones Juris Canonici*, I, 253; Vermeersch-Creusen, *Epitome*, III, 395; Cocchi, *Commentarium*, VI, 81.

[32] Micheletti, *op. cit.*, p. 40.

[33] Vermeersch-Creusen, *Epitome*, loc. cit.

Priesthood, and the necessity of constant training in virtue, prayer, and all things that tend to nourish the spiritual life of man. In a seminary, proper provisions are made for both intellectual training and spiritual development. Moreover, the moral union of a community life, in which all the members are imbued with the one desire to become worthy priests, is one of the best means to cherish and to protect vocations.[34] Now, as in every age, the strident voice of the world seeks to deafen the ears of men to the plea of Jesus Christ, calling them to His ministry. The Church, therefore, not only permits, but strongly advises the enrollment of students who are still quite young. Once admitted to the seminary, a student has the advantage of seclusion from mundane distractions, and of a course of studies coordinated to the one end of fitting him for the Priesthood. And while there he has the inestimable privilege of living under the same roof with the eternal Priest, Jesus Christ. These considerations remove any exaggeration from the statement that seminaries are an indispensable foundation for true ecclesiastical discipline.[35] A well trained priesthood is a guarantee of a well instructed laity,[36] and since the seminarian is the future priest,[37] it has been aptly stated that a good seminary is the best guarantee of a good diocese.[38]

---

[34] Leo XIII, encycl. "*Quod multum,*" Aug. 22, 1886, Fontes, n. 594; Themistor, *L'Instruction et l'Education du clergé,* p. 35.

[35] . . . "stare ecclesiastica disciplina sine illorum subsidio ac adminiculo vix possit," Conc. Aquila (1596)—Harduin, X, 1904.

[36] "Talis populus, qualis sacerdos"—Micheletti, *De Regimine,* p. 41.

[37] "Quales in seminario alumni, tales in ministerio presbyteri," Conc. Burdig. tit. V, c. 1, apud Micheletti, *op. cit.*, p. 271.

[38] Micheletti, *op. cit.*, p. 41.

CHAPTER TWO

1.—*The First Centuries of the Church*

Our Divine Lord instituted His Church to conserve and propagate His teaching to the end of time. He entrusted its government to His Apostles, who had been His constant companions during the years of His public life. They had talked with Him concerning the mysteries of His kingdom, and had drunk deep from the Fountain of eternal wisdom, although it was not until Pentecost that they realized the full meaning of His words and the value of His doctrine. The Apostles, then, were prepared for their momentous mission by the oral teaching of Christ Himself. However, the permanent character of the Church and of the Christian Priesthood demanded that others succeed them in the sacred ministry, and it is with the Apostles themselves that the tradition begins that it is the right and duty of the Bishop personally to instruct candidates for the Priesthood. With the growth of the Church, this right of episcopal supervision was necessarily exercised through the medium of others, but the principle has ever been maintained, and underlies all legislation on clerical education.

There is no legislation on this subject during the first three centuries of Christianity, but there is no doubt that the principle of episcopal supervision was generally recognized and followed. The power of ordination rested within the hands of the Bishops, and there was a concomitant duty to impose hands on none but worthy candidates. St. Paul[1] exhorted Timothy to exert great care in the matter of ordinations, demanding that the candidate be proved worthy of the office of the Priesthood. The implication is that there should be some period of special training, and its actual existence may be inferred from the institution of minor orders.[2] Besides a knowledge of the life and doctrine of Christ, the candidate was required to discharge the functions of each of these minor offices. This enabled

[1] "Hi autem probentur et sic minstrent"—*I Ep. to Timothy*, III, 10; Idem, V, 22.

[2] Thomassinus, *Nova et Vestus Disciplina Ecclesiae*, II, I, c. 101, n. 1.

him to acquire a practical knowledge of the priestly ministry, and afforded the Bishop an opportunity to further instruct him in Christian doctrine and to judge of his qualities and aptitude.[3] Historians and canonists alike[4] are agreed not only concerning the existence of this period of clerical training, but also that it was carried on under the immedate supervision of the Bishop. Moreover, the grace of God was operating in an extraordinary manner during the Apostolic period, and this often precluded the necessity of formal theological training. Many of those who first entered the clerical state possessed the various charismata, and the active operation of the Holy Ghost in the infant Church certainly supplied many defects in the intellectual attainments of her ministers.[5] In the following two centuries the periodic persecutions to which Christianity was subjected rendered it impossible to have any large congregations of clerics,[6] and the number of both priests and clerics was usually very small.[7]

The rise of the catechetical schools marked a development in general education, and proved a valuable adjunct to clerical education. They developed into centers of theological discussion,[8] and many who later became Bishops and priests received an intensive training there in Christian doctrine and thought.[9] The principal catechetical schools were founded at important centers of culture, such as Alexandria, Caesarea, Antioch, Edessa, and Nisibus. However, while these institutions undoubtedly afforded an opportunity for greater intellectual progress in the study of Christian doctrine, their importance for clerical education should not be exaggerated. There was

---

[3] Probst, *Kirchliche Disciplin*, p. 73; Alzog, *Universal Church History*, I, 395.

[4] Brueck, *History of the Church*, I, 70; Marcault, *L'Education des Clercs*, p. 67; Vieban, art. "Seminary," Catholic Encyc., XIII, 694; Icard, *Traditions de St. Sulpice*, p. 2; Badii, *Institutiones Juris Canonici*, II, 147; "Clerici etiam juniores ab ipso episcopo aut saltem sub ejus directione erudiri solebant."—Wernz, *Jus Decretalium*, III, n. 92; A. J. P., XI, 420.

[5] I Cor., c. 12; Moran, *Government of the Church in the First Century*, p. 255.

[6] Wernz, *Jus Decretalium*, III, n. 92; Thomassinus, *op. cit.*, I, III, c. 2, n. 1; Badii, *op. cit.*, II, 47; Benedict XIV, *De Synodo*, V, c. 11, n. 1.

[7] Bouix, *De Capitulis*, p. 3; Thomassinus, *op. cit.*, I, III, c. 7, n. 2.

[8] Schmidt, *Geschichte der Pedagogik*, II, 41; Ayer, art. "*Catechetical Schools*," Encyclopedia of Education, I, 546; Thomassinus, *op. cit.*, II, I, c. 92, n. 1; Lexikon der Pedagogik, v. "*Katechetenschule*," II, 1115.

[9] Zallwein, *Principia Juris Ecclesiastici*, IV, 245; Probst, *Lehre und Gebet in den drei Ersten Christlichen Jahrhunderten*, pp. 182-83; Schrődl, art. "*Séminaire*," *Dictionnaire de la Théologie*, XXI, 480; Schaff, *History of the Christian Church*, II, 257.

no community life, and no pretensions to being clerical schools. Only a minority of future priests attended them, and they could not supplant the training given under the Bishops, for even though the latter approved of them and sometimes took measures to prevent heterodox teaching in them,[10] there was still a necessity for spiritual formation under episcopal supervision.

2.—*From the Fourth to the Eighth Century*

The dawn of the fourth century inaugurated a new era in the history of the Christian Church. Under the aegis of royal toleration conditions became much more favorable for the propagation of the faith and the foundation of Christian institutions. The activities of the Church received wider scope and greater impetus, and legislation concerning clerical discipline became frequent. There are many indications that indirectly attest to the existence of a formative period of clerical training. Candidates for ordination to the Priesthood were required to be of mature age,[11] usually stated at thirty years; Bishops were forbidden to ordain candidates who were unknown to them,[12] or who had recently been converted.[13] Ordinations *per saltum,* by the omission of any one of the minor orders, was strictly prohibited,[14] and Pope Leo I appealed to their institution as the most ancient tradition in the probation of candidates for the priesthood.[15] Moreover, both in ecclesiastical legislation[16] and in Roman law,[17] a knowledge of Christian doctrine and law, and even of profane letters, was required for ordination. From the end of the fourth century on, this requisite knowledge and training was acquired either in the monastic schools, or in one or other of the various types of non-monastic schools.

---

[10] Duchesne, *History of the Christian Church,* p. 247.

[11] Codex Justinianus (a. 390) I, 3, 9; Council of Neo-Caesarea (a. 446), c. 11—c. 4, D. LXXVIII; Conc. Agde (a. 506) c. 16—c. 6, D. LXXVII; Fourth Council of Toledo (a. 633) c. 20—c. 7, D. LXXVII; Council of Hippo (a. 393) c. 1—Hefele, Conciliengeschichte, II, 56.

[12] Council of Sardica (a. 343) c. 18—Hefele, *op. cit.*, I, 598; Council of Chalcedon (a. 451) c. 20—c. 3, D. LXXI; Letter of Pope Siricuis to Himericus—Harduin I, 856.

[13] Synod of Laodicea (a. 360) c. 3—Hefele, *op. cit.*, I, 752.

[14] Council of Sardica (a. 343) c. 10—Hefele, *op. cit.*, I, 590; Pope Zosimus, Ep. to Hesychius (a. 418)—c. 2, D. LXXIX; Pope Celestine to Gallic Bishops (a. 428)—c. 4, D. LXXIX; Pope Gelasius—c. 1, D. LXXVII.

[15] Pope Leo I, *Ep. to the Bishops of Africa*—M. P. L., LIV, 649.

[16] Third Council of Carthage (a. 397) c. 22—c. 3, D. XXIV; Pope Zosimus, Ep. to Hesychius (a. 418)—c. 1, D. LIX.

[17] Novellae, CXXIII, 12; VI, 4, 15; VI, 1, 7.

Monastic Schools

Monasticism, which had originated toward the end of the third century in the deserts of Egypt,[18] was brought to the West by St. Athanasius.[19] The primary purpose of the monastic system was the development and cultivation of spirituality by means of prayer and seclusion, but the educational activities of the monks soon rendered their schools important factors in clerical education.[20] There were two classes of monastic schools: [21]

1. The *interior* or *conventual* school, in which aspirants to the monastic state were educated. They were also called *claustral* schools, and the pupils were styled *oblati*.

2. The *exterior* or *secular* school, in which candidates for the secular priesthood, together with lay students, were taught. The pupils were called *nutriti*.

After the general adoption of the Benedictine rule,[22] a further division into major and minor schools existed in most monasteries.[23] In the latter were taught the fundamentals of Christian doctrine, chant, arithmetic, grammar, etc.; in the former, theology and Sacred Scripture. This presents a striking analogy to the present system of major and minor seminaries.

Non-Monastic Schools

The history of the non-monastic schools is closely related to that of community life among the diocesan clergy. In the early ages of the Church, each Bishop was aided in the administration of his diocese by a *presbyterium*, constisting of priests and deacons,[24] who remained with him whenever and as far as circumstances allowed. Community life among the clergy, however, was necessarily difficult, and in many cases was completely abandoned during the ages of persecution. The revival of this important phase of clerical disci-

---

[18] Montalembert, *Monks of the West*, I, 225.

[19] Montalembert, *op. cit.*, I, 286.

[20] Dubourguier, *Grandes Ecoles et Gens d'Eglise*, p. 36; Maitre, *Les Ecoles Episcopales et Monastiques*, p. 118; McCormick, *History of Education*, p. 89.

[21] "Erant ergo in coenobiis nostris scholae interiores seu claustrales pro monachis, exteriores seu canonicae pro saecularibus."—Mabillon, *Acta SS. O. S. B., Praef. in saec. III*, p. 98, n. 3; Benedict XIV, *De Synodo*, V, c. 11, n. 2; Mabillon, *Traittes des Etudes*, p. 51; Dubourguier, *op. cit.*, p. 48; Robert, *Les Ecoles et l'Enseignement du Moitie de XIII Siècle*, p. 17.

[22] Mabillon, *Acta SS. O. S. B.*, Praef. in saec. III, n. 4, p. 171; Council of Leptine (a. 747)—Harduin, 3, 1921; Council of Rouen (a. 1074)—Mansi, 20, 399.

[23] Mabillon, *op. cit.*, *Praef. in saec. IV*, p. 286, n. 184.

[24] Bouix, *De Capitulis*, p. 3; Wernz-Vidal, *De Personis*, n. 654.

pline is attributed to St. Augustine, who perfected it and organized it under definite regulations.[25] Realizing the value of a close bond or moral union among his diocesan clergy, he organized a community consisting of the priests, deacons, and subdeacons attached to his diocese. These lived together in the episcopal residence under his supervision, partook of the same table, dressed alike, and performed their spiritual exercises in common. All were bound by the vow of poverty.[26] This community of St. Augustine is generally considered to be the progenitor of the system of episcopal and cathedral schools, and it the first historical evidence of any institute resembling our modern seminary.[27] The restriction of membership in the community to clerics above the subdiaconate, and the compulsory vow of poverty, however, present substantial differences between the institute of the saintly Bishop of Hippo and the seminary of the Council of Trent.

The system inaugurated by St. Augustine was adopted by many of the neighboring Bishops, and the dispersion of the African Church during the Vandal invasions caused it to be carried to Europe.[28] This, then, marks the origin of the episcopal school, which was designated in ecclesiastical legislation by the term *episcopia*. The clerics lived in common, either in the episcopal residence or at least, nearby,[29] and were taught by the Bishop himself or by someone appointed by him, very often a member of a monastic order.[30] The second Council of Tours (a. 523)[31] indicated that the system of episcopal schools was widespread in Gaul during the fifth and sixth centuries, and the same is true of Spain.[32] A century later, the fourth Council

[25] Hinschius, *System des Katholischen Kirchenrechts*, II, 50; Wernz-Vidal, *op. cit.*, loc. cit.; St. Augustine, *Sermo CCCLV*, M. P. L. XXXIX, 1568; *Sermo CCCLVI*, Idem, XXXIX, 1574.

[26] Possidius, *Vita S. Augustini*—M. P. L. XXXII, 37, 54, 174; Pouan, *De Seminario Clericorum*, p. 21.

[27] Theiner, *Histoire des Institutions d'Education Ecclesiastique*, p. 107; Leclercq, art. "*Ecole*," Dictionnaire d'Archaeologie Chrétienne (Cabrol), IV, 1832; Schmidt, *Geschichte der Pedagogik*, II, 66-67; Lexikon der Pedagogik, v. "Augustine," I, 298; Benedict XIV, *De Synodo*, V, c. 11, n. 1; Cecco, *Instituzioni dei Seminari Vescovili*, p. 10.

[28] Theiner, *op. cit.*, pp. 111-115; Alzog, *Universal Church History*, II, 29; Trezzini, *La Legislazione Canonica di Gelasio*, I, p. 45.

[29] Thomassinus, *Nova et Vetus Disciplina Ecclesiae*, I, III, c. 8, n. 1; Van Espen, *Jus Ecclesiasticum Universum*, II, 1, 9, 1; A. J. P., III, 282.

[30] Mabillon, *Acta SS. O. S. B., Praef. in saec. III*, p. 93, n. 3; Idem, *op. cit.*, n. 46; Themistor, *L'Instruction et l'Education du clergé*, p. 31; Maitre, *op. cit.*, p. 125.

[31] C. 12—Mansi, IX, 790.

[32] Second Council of Toledo (a. 531) c. 1—Mansi, VIII, 785.

of Toledo (a. 631) [33] confirmed the necessity of the episcopal school, and further prescribed the erection of an auxiliary institute, outside the episcopal palace, in which the more youthful clerics should be taught and trained under the guidance of an approved senior priest. This seems to be the first ecclesiastical legislation concerning the constitution of a minor school for more youthful aspirants to the ecclesiastical state.

Pope Gregory I, about the beginning of the seventh century, instituted at Rome a community somewhat similar to that of St. Augustine, which exhibited in its educational activities some of the characteristics of both the episcopal and monastic schools. The community was attached to the cathedral Church of Rome, the Lateran, and hence was called the "Patriarchate of the Lateran." Within its walls, the older clergy were entrusted with the task of teaching the clerics both sacred science and literature, and it numbered among its student members not only the youth of Rome but also of other Christian provinces.[34] This then, was the first Pontifical seminary. Duchesne [35] also mentions the organization of clerics in minor orders into the so-called *scholae cantorum.* These were adjuncts to the Lateran seminary, and the students lived in common under the supervision of a superior who taught them ecclesiastical chant, literature, and the fundamentals of Christian doctrine.[36] The institution of the minor schools thus far mentioned indicates the constant desire of the Church to begin the training of prospective clerics from their early youth.

In many cases, however, as in rural parishes, it was not feasible for clerical students to attend either the episcopal or monastic schools. The only solution was the institution of the *rectory* schools in individual parishes, where the student was taught by the pastor. The latter was usually assisted in the various parochial functions by clerics in minor orders, who at the same time lived a community life under his guidance and training.[37] The Rectory schools were

[33] C. 24—Mansi, X, 626.

[34] Thomassinus, *Nova et Vetus Disciplina Ecclesiae,* I, II, c. 14, n. 7; Joly, *Traittes Historiques,* pp. 93-94; A. J. P., I., 654-55; Theiner, *Institutions d'Education Ecclésiastique,* p. 119; Andrieu, art. "*Les Ordres Mineurs dans l'ancien Rit Romain,*" Revue des Sciences Réligieuses, V, pp. 234-37; Pius X, Const., "*In praecipuis,*" June 29, 1913—A. A. S. (1913), 297.

[35] *Liber Pontificalis,* I, 321-22; Idem, *Origines due Culte Chrétien,* pp. 368-69.

[36] Joly, *op. cit.,* p. 94.

[37] Bastnagel, *The Appointment of Parochial Adjutants and Assistants,* p. 22; *Revue des Sciences Réligieuses,* V, 234.

at least inchoate seminaries, in which the student received either the full course of training and education for the Priesthood, or a partial training until such time as circumstances permitted attendance at the episcopal institute.[38] The Council of Vaison (a. 529) [39] urged their erection in Gaul, and cited the example of Italy, where they had evidently existed successfully for some time. The Council of Merida, in Spain, (a. 666) [40] attests to the continued growth of the rectory school system during the seventh century. Besides ordering the institution of rectory schools, the Council also provided that the pastor should provide for the material necessities of the students. The Council of Vaison (a. 755) endeavored to restrict them to students who had not yet entered the clerical state by decreeing that all tonsured clerics should live and study either in a monastic community of episcopal school.[41] The importance of the rectory schools cannot be overestimated, for they served the cause of clerical education even during periods of decadence in the episcopal school system.

3.—*From the Reign of Charlemagne to the Universities*

Social disorders and the barbarian invasions caused a general decline in clerical education toward the end of the seventh century,[42] and there was no reform until after the accession of the Carolingian dynasty.[43] In Germany, the observance of community life among the diocesan clergy was revived and propagated by Chrodegang, Bishop of Metz.[44] To secure this end he utilized the principles of community life promulgated by St. Augustine, together with an adaptation of the Benedictine rule to the life of the secular clergy. This revival of communal life greatly facilitated the education and training of clerical students.[45] The schools attached to such com-

---

38 Thomassinus, *op. cit.*, I, III, c. 6, n. 6; Vita S. Launomauri, *Acta SS. O. S. B.*, I, 317.

39 C. 1—Mansi, VIII, 726.

40 C. 17—Mansi, IX, 85.

41 C. 11—Mansi, XII, 582.

42 Dubourguier, *Grandes Ecoles et Gens d'Eglise*, p. 34.

43 West, "Alcuin," p. 41; Maitre, *Les Ecoles Episcopales et Monastiques*, p. 117; Gaskoin, v. "*Charlemagne*," Encyclopedia of Education, I, 578; Themistor, *L'Instruction et l'Education du clergé*, p. 31.

44 Hinschius, *System des Katholischen Kirchenrechts*, II, 52 ss.; Wernz-Vidal, *De Personis*, II, n. 654; Mansi, XIV, 315-31; Harduin, IV, 1181-98; Thomassinus, *op. cit.*, II, I, c. 101, n. 1.

45 Theiner, *Institutions d'Education Ecclésiastique*, p. 134; Pouan, *De Seminario Clericorum*, pp. 47-49; Stockl, *Lehrbuch der Geschichte der Pedagogik*, p. 109; Maitre, *op. cit.*, p. 126.

munities were usually called *cathedral* or *canonical* schools. They were practically the same as the episcopal schools, and were merely the result of better clerical organization in diocesan centers. Both were comprised by the same canonical term *episcopia*.

The Emperor Charlemagne introduced a period of unprecedented activity in the field of education.[46] Besides a general revival of letters and culture, there was a systematic promotion of the cause of clerical education by means of both imperial capitularies and conciliar decrees. The first of these important enactments was the famous capitulary *Constitutio de scholis per singula episcopia et monasteria instituendis*, issued in the year 788.[47] The Council of Aix-la-Chapelle, in 789,[48] ordered Bishops to subject their ordinands to a severe examination before ordaining them and demanded the institution of minor schools in every monastery and episcopal residence.[49] Clerics were compelled to attend either a cathedral or monastic school until they had passed a stringent examination, and were deemed worthy of promotion to the Priesthood; and they could not be ordained before the age of thirty.[50] The capitularies of Charlemagne and his successors were renewed, and the system of Chrodegang was approved, by many councils.[51] The Bishops, of course, exercised supervision over all communities of secular clerics,[52] and the Council of Aix-la-Chappelle, in 816, dwelt at great length on the qualities requisite for the various major and minor orders, in order that the Bishops might have a definite norm to guide them in their selection of candidates for ordination.[53] The rectory schools still continued to serve the cause of clerical education,[54] especially when the political chaos resulting from the Norman

[46] Maitre, *op. cit.*, p. 117; Themistor, *L'Instruction et l'Education du Clergé*, p. 31; Dubourguier, *Grandes Ecoles et Gens d'Eglise*, p. 38; West, *op. cit.*, p. 45.

[47] Mansi, XVII b, 201-04.

[48] C. 2—Mansi, XVII b, 214.

[49] C. 70—Mansi, XVII b, 237.

[50] Capitulary (a. 802) c. 22, Mansi, XVII b, 369; Capitulary (a. 803) c. 2, Mansi, XVII b, 391; Third Council of Tours (a. 813) c. 12, Harduin, IV, 1025.

[51] Council of Mayence (a. 813) c. 9—Mansi, XIV, 67; Council of Chalons sur Saone (a. 813) c. 3—Mansi, XIV, 94; Council of Meaux (a. 836) c. 78—Mansi, XIV, 840; Council of Valence (a. 855) c. 18—Mansi, XV, 11; Council of Touls (a. 859) c. 10—Mansi, XV, 539.

[52] Council of Aix-la-Chapelle (a. 836) c. 1—Mansi, XIV, 679.

[53] cc. 2 to 23—Mansi, XIV, 154-82.

[54] Sixth Council of Paris (a. 829) c. 2, Harduin IV, 1316; Capitulary of Walter, Archbishop of Arles (a. 858)—Mansi, XV, 506; Liber Legum Ecclesiasticarum, Mansi, XIX, 184, 246.

invasions and the break-up of the feudal system had caused a general decline in the cathedral and monastic schools.

4.—From the Universities to the Council of Trent

Universities were not instituted primarily as institutes of clerical education, yet they have exerted an important influence upon it. Faculties of Theology and Canon Law became distinctive features of their curriculum, especially at the University of Paris, and a majority of those who attended the universities were clerics. The formation of scholastic theology, the coordination of the ecclesiastical canons in the Decretals, the reputation of famous teachers in ecclesiastical science, all combined to attract clerical students from all over the world. For some time the local schools were hopelessly unable to compete with the course of studies given at the Universities, and there was a consequent trend toward these latter centers of learning which resulted in the decadence and almost total disappearance of the episcopal schools.[55] There can be no question of the superiority of the university curriculum. However, the universities did not foster piety and clerical discipline as zealously as they promoted intellectual progress.[56] The foundation of hospices and religious college houses[57] helped in some measure to supply the lack of well organized clerical life and competent supervision, and also provided for the education and sustenance of some of the poorer clerical students, but not even the quasi-community life of these institutions prevented a general spirit of laxity. The consensus of opinion is that the universities did not have a beneficial effect on clerical education in general, and this contention is borne out by the legislation of the period.

The Council of Rheims (a. 1131) condemned monks and canons for studying law and medicine at the Universities instead of theology,[58] and severe penalties were incurred not only by the guilty clerics, but also by their superiors. The Second Council of the

[55] Dubourguier, *Grandes Ecoles et Gens d'Eglise*, p. 301; Eiselt, art. "*Ecoles des Cathédrales*," Dictionnaire Théologique, VII, 86; Robert, *L'Ecoles et l'Enseignement du Moitié de XII Siècle*, pp. 10-11; *Les Ecoles Episcopales et Monastiques*, p. 113; Theiner, *L'Instruction et l'Education du Clergé*, p. 185; Thomassinus, *Nova et Vetus Disciplina Ecclesiae*, II, I, c. 102, n. 1.

[56] Thomassinus, *op. cit.*, II, I, c. 101, n. 1-2; Marcault, *L'Education des Clercs*, p. 147; Bingham. *Christian Antiquities*, VI, c. V, n. 5; Bonal, *Institutiones Canonicae*, II, 222: Wernz, *Jus Decretalium*, III, n. 92.

[57] Thomassinus, *op. cit.*. II, I, c. 102, n. 1; Wernz, *loc. cit.*; A. J. P., I, 662.

[58] C. 9—Mansi, XXI, 528.

Lateran (a. 1139),[59] and the Council of Tours (a. 1163),[60] imposed the penalty of excommunication upon the clerics if they did not return to their monastery or canonical community within two months, and the abbots or piors permitting such an abuse were to be deprived of their honors and were also subject to excommunication. The Council of Paris (a. 1212)[61] stated that many monks and clerics were attending the Universities from motives of mere pride or curiosity, and that they should pursue studies congruent to their state within their own communities. Determined efforts were made by both Popes and Councils to foster episcopal schools for the majority of clerical students. Thus the Third Council of the Lateran (a. 1179), under Pope Alexander III, decreed the erection of a clerical school in every cathederal city,[62] and this legislation was confirmed by the Fourth Council of the Lateran (a. 1215),[63] and by the Council of Basle (a. 1431).[64] The latter Council was the last prior to the beginning of the sixteenth century to make any determined effort in the interest of clerical education.

5.—*Officials of Clerical Schools before the Council of Trent*

The absence of any definite legislation on the subject indicates that the regulations governing the interior administration of clerical schools were left to the discretion of the Bishops and religious Superiors. The actual supervision of clerical training was usually entrusted to a diocesan official, and some enactments exist prior to the Council of Trent pertinent to the duties of the officials who, from time to time, discharged this office. In the early ages of the Church it was the duty of the archdeacon,[65] who probably took an active part in the training of clerics studying in the episcopal residence, and maintained a vigilant watch over the training given in the rectory schools.[66] Hinschius[67] asserts that the *primicerius* often undertook the actual education of the younger clerics, especially in matters pertinent to the practice of the ministry, as in liturgy and

[59] C. 9—Mansi, XXI, 528.
[60] C. 8—Mansi, XXI, 1179.
[61] C. 10—Mansi, XXII, 831.
[62] C. 18—Mansi, XXII, 228.
[63] C. 11—Mansi, XXII, 999.
[64] C. 3—Harduin, VIII, 1248.
[65] "Clericorum minorum dux erat ille et rector et magister. . . ."—Thomassinus, *Nova et Vetus Disciplina Ecclesiae*, I, II, c. 17.
[66] C. 1, X, *De officio archdiaconi*, I, 23.
[67] *System des Katholischen Kirchenrechts*, II, 97.

chant. He exercised a sort of extra-judicial authority with reference to the direction, monition, and correction if the students, and the maintenance of discipline among them.[68] The rule of Chrodegang prescribed that the archdeacon and primicerius be well versed in the Scriptures and the sacred canons, in order that they might be fitted to teach the clerics,[69] and the primicerius often taught letters and grammar.[70] Up to the ninth century, however, such indefinite terms as *minister, probatissimus senior,* and *vitae probabilis frater* were sometimes used to designate ecclesiastical teachers.[71]

Gradually the duty of teaching in the cathedral and episcopal schools devolved upon the canon deemed to possess the best qualifications for it, and he was given the title of *scholasticus.*[72] At first this was a mere office, but later it was raised to a benefice, and even to a dignity.[73] These benefices were called *scholasteriae.* The number of clerical students often necessitated the appointment of assistant teachers, who were usually called *magistri.*[74] The latter term came into general use after the origin of the universities, and was considered synonymous with *professor.*[75] The term *scholasticus* was also applied to the monks who discharged the teaching office in the monastery schools. In the event that a capable teacher could not be found among the monks attached to a monastery, it was customary for the superior to apply to another monastery for a monk who could fill the office.[76] Very often the office of scholasticus in the episcopal schools was bestowed on a member of a religious order.[77]

There was little legislation concerning the teachers prior to the twelfth century. The Council of Paris (a. 824) ordered Bishops

---

[68] Bouix, *De Capitulis,* p. 117; Van-Espen, *Jus Ecclesiasticum Universum,* I, XI, c. 3; c. un., X, *De officio Primicerii,* I, 25.

[69] Harduin, IV, 1192; Hinschius, *op. cit.,* p. 110; Barbosa, *De Canonicis,* IX, n. 6.

[70] Joly, *Traittes Historiques des Ecoles Episcopales,* p. 164.

[71] Council of Aix-la-Chapelle (a. 836) c. 12—Mansi, XIV, 679; Fourth Council of Toledo (a. 633), c. 14—Mansi, X, 626; Rule of Chrodegang—Labbaeus, IX, 490.

[72] Zallwein, *Principia Juris Ecclesiastici,* IV, 246; Hinschius, *op. cit.,* II, 100; Van Espen, *op. cit.,* I, XI, c. 4; Mansi, XIV, 484.

[73] Van Espen, loc. cit.; Hinschius, *op. cit.,* II, 102; Maitre, *Les Ecoles Episcopales et Monastiques,* p. 126.

[74] Council of Mayence (a. 813) c. 9—Harduin, IV, 1011; Hinschius, *op. cit.,* II, 101.

[75] Rashdall, *Universities in the Middle Ages,* I, 21; Themistor, *L'Instruction et l'Education du Clergé,* p. 32; cc. 1-5, X, De magistris, V. 5.

[76] Mabillon, *Acta SS. O.S.B., Praef. in saec. IV,* n. 184.

[77] Mabillon, *op. cit., Praef in saec. III,* n. 46.

to bring their scholastics to the various provincial Councils in order to promote the cause of clerical education.[78] Pope Leo IV decreed that professors should make an annual report to the Bishop.[79] The *scholasticus* had the privilege of selecting those who were to act as his assistants in teaching. The right to teach should have been accorded gratuitously to these assistant professors, but in both England and France the abuse arose of exacting from them a sum of money before granting them the license to teach. The Council of London (a. 1138) [80] severely reprobated this venality, and Pope Alexander III, in a letter to the Bishops of France, reprehended the practice and decreed deposition and deprivation of office and benefices for those guilty of it.[81] This same prohibition was incorporated in the canons of the Third Council of the Lateran.[82]

At the same time, the problem of providing some appropriate remuneration for professors demanded solution, and the Third Council of the Lateran, for the first time, assigned a benefice to those who taught in clerical schools.[83] The Council mentions not only episcopal schools, but also decrees the restoration of magistri in all schools and monasteries where education had formerly been imparted. The decrees of the Council, which were later renewed in their entirety by Pope Innocent III, in the Fourth Lateran Council,[84] are as follows:

1. A professor of letters must be chosen in every cathedral and collegiate church by the Bishop thereof, with the consent of the chapter.

2. In metropolitan churches, a professor of theology must also be appointed, and even in other churches, if they could support one.

3. To both these offices was assigned the revenue from one prebend.

4. These professors were not thereby made canons of the chapter.

5. If the sequestration of a prebend for this purpose should prove onerous, then some portion of the revenues of one should be given to the theologian, and the professor of letters could then be supported by contributions from other diocesan churches.

---

[78] C. 30—Mansi, XVII b, 1137.

[79] Synod of Rome (a. 853) n. 34—Mansi, XIV, 1014.

[80] C. 17—Harduin, VI, pt. 2, 1206.

[81] (a. 1170), c. 3, X, *De magistris*, V, 5; Harduin XIV b, 1470; Robert, *L'Enseignement du Moitié de XIII Siècle*, pp. 32-34.

[82] C. 18—Mansi XXII, 228.

[83] Mansi, *loc. cit.*

[84] (a. 1215) c. 4, X, *De magistris*, V, 5; Giraldi, *Expositio Juris Pontificii*, II, 594; Thomassinus, *Nova et Vetus Disciplina Ecclesiae*, I, II, c. 10, n. .

The famous decree of Pope Honorius III, "*Super specula*," issued in 1219,[85] reiterated and demanded the observance of the Lateran legislation. It further endeavored to facilitate its execution by providing for the selection of promising and apt clerics to pursue the study of theology in the universities. These men were presumably to return at the completion of their course to teach in their respective local schools. This was a tacit recognition of the wider scope and more thorough character of the university curriculum, and shows at the same time that a system of local cathedral schools was necessary to ensure the proper training for the greater number of clerical students. Those engaged in the study of theology at the universities were exempt from the law of residence and continued to receive the revenue from their prebend, although they were not entitled to the daily distributions.[86] The Council of Buda (a. 1279) [87] extended this privilege of exemption from residence to students of Canon Law. It also provided that the archdeacon should spend at least three years in the study of Canon Law. The Council of Basle (a. 1431) required that a professor of theology should have at least a baccalaureate in theology, and that he should have studied at least ten years in a university.[88] This decree was renewed by Pope Leo X, in a concordat with the Emperor Francis.[89]

Thus concludes a period of important and constructive legislation for the advancement of clerical education. All the enactments refer, however, to the teaching office. There seems to have been no separate and definite legislation concerning the economic administration of the various schools, and presumably this was provided for in the general administration of diocesan temporalities. The Council of Tours (a. 813) intimates that the Bishop provided for the material necessities of the clerics who studied in the episcopal school.[90] The Archdeacon probably performed this function in the canonicate schools.

[85] C. 5, X, *De magistris*, V, 5.
[86] C. 12, X, *De clericis non residentibus*, III, 4; c. 32, X, *De praebendis*, III, 5; c. 5, X, *De magistris*, V, 5.
[87] C. 28—Mansi, XXIV, 287.
[88] C. 3—Mansi, XXIX, 163-64.
[89] Mansi, XXXII, 1023.
[90] C. 23—Mansi, XIV, 86.

CHAPTER THREE

1.—*The Immediate Pre-Tridentine Period*

The important and constructive legislation of the preceding two centuries was generally disregarded by the beginning of the sixteenth century.[1] The legislative enactments of the period indicate a general decadence of institutes for clerical training. An earnest endeavor was made by positive legislation to render the requirements for ordination more stringent and to ensure their observance by those whose duty it was to present the candidates. Their failure is evident from the fact that, even in the sixteenth century, many priests could not read nor speak Latin, and it was found necessary to legislate that they at least be able to interpret the sacred Scriptures.[2] This type of legislation culminated in a demand by the Council of Sienna (1528) that all those already ordained should be examined, and suspension was decreed for those priests who were found deficient.[3] Most of the cathedral and episcopal schools had disappeared, due to the influence of the universities.[4]

The Council of Cologne, in 1549, decreed that the literary studies which we associate with the curriculum of a minor seminary should be pursued by the students under the tutelage of their respective pastors, whether in the city or in the country.[5] It then goes on to say that courses in philosophy, law, theology, and Sacred Scripture could be expected only in the universities approved by the Church, although some theology might be obtained in some of the richer monasteries and collegiate schools.[6] The obvious inference is that

---

[1] Cf. Council of Cologne (1536) c. 3, Mansi, 32, 1285.

[2] Council of Sienna (1485)—Mansi, 32, 417; Council of Toledo (1473) c. 3—Mansi, 32, 385; Conc. Seville (1512)—Mansi, 32, 609.

[3] C. 6—Mansi, 32, 1186.

[4] A. J. P., I, 633; Theiner, *Histoire des Institutions d'Education Ecclésiastique*, p. 188.

[5] C. II—Mansi, 32, 1364 ss.

[6] " . . . reliqua philosophia . . . jurisprudentia et theologia seu Scriptura Sacra nonnisi in probatis academiis et catholicis studiorum scholis exspectentur, doceantur, ac tradantur; nisi quod theologia etiam in monasteriis opulentioribus ac collegiis canonicorum debeat doceri . . . "—Mansi, 32, 1365; Thomassinus, *Nova et Vetus Disciplina Ecclesiae*, II, I, 101, n. 8.

only in the universities and richer institutes could a proper training in theology be received by the candidate for the Priesthood. The Church was once more confronted with the necessity for drastic reform measures. Pope Paul III appointed a commission of nine cardinals in 1538 to consider the question of clerical reform, and the first measure proposed by them was the general restoration of the Cathedral schools.[7] This proposal was reiterated by the Emperor Charles V before the Diet of Augsburg, in 1541. These suggestions, often previously made in vain, were soon followed by the erection of the German College at Rome by St. Ignatius. Pope Julius III issued the Bull of erection in 1552,[8] and Pope Gregory XIII officially published its constitutions in 1584.[9] From this institution blazed forth the beacon light of common life, austere discipline, and the cultivation of the sciences of theology and the liberal arts—a light which guided the Fathers of the Council of Trent in their deliberations on clerical training, and won for St. Ignatius the title of "Precursor" of the clerical reformation.[10]

The most important legislation of this period was a decree on clerical education issued by Reginald Cardinal Pole, one of the most prominent English churchmen during this critical period. He was a member of the above mentioned commission which was appointed by Pope Paul III to consider church reforms, and was one of the three Papal legates first appointed to preside over the Council of Trent. He later succeeded Archbishop Cranmer as Primate of England, and labored zealously for the reorganization of the Church in England.[11]

It was during this latter period that he promulgated the decree above mentioned, which was later amplified and incorporated in the legislation of Trent. The analogy between the two laws is strikingly summarized by Thomassinus: "We are forced to confess that these two are so related and so similar that either Cardinal Pole presumed those things upon which the Fathers of Trent were meditating, or else they afterwards merely complemented those things which Pole had begun." [12]

---

[7] A. J. P., I, 633.
[8] Aug. 31, 1552—Bullarium Romanum, VI, 459-62.
[9] May 1, 1584—Bullarium Romanum, VIII, 477-55.
[10] Marcault, *L'Education des Clercs*, pp. 152-54; Vieban, art. "*Seminary*," Catholic Encyclopedia, XIII, 694-702; Theiner, *Histoire des Institutions d'Education Ecclésiastique*, pp. 201-05.
[11] Thurston, art. "*Cardinal Pole*," Catholic Encyclopedia, XII, 201-03.
[12] *Nova et Vetus Disciplina Ecclesiae*, II, I, c. 102, n. 10.

This fact is evident from a comparative analysis. The following is a summary of the legislation promulgated by the Cardinal, February 9, 1556:

1. No other more seemly remedy could be found for the paucity of clerics fitted to discharge their office than the institution of seminaries.

2. The requirements for entrance are that the candidate be at least eleven years of age, able to read and write, and possessed of a character that affords hope of a fruitful ministry in the priesthood.

3. The children of the poor are to be preferred, although those of the rich are not to be excluded.

4. After a preparatory education in the liberal arts, the candidates can then be admitted to the cathedral school, where they are to be taught the ecclesiastical sciences by the chancellor or some other competent teacher. The older students are to receive their sustenance and clothing, and a yearly stipend besides; the junior students receive only board and clothing. All, however, are to live in common and wear the clerical tonsure. After a sufficient course of study the candidate is to be ordained, and assigned to any office the Bishop may deem fit.

5. Other youths may be admitted to these schools, even though they do not intend to study for the priesthood. They must conform in all things to the other students.

6. The maintenance of the seminary will be provided for by a tax levied on the revenues of the Bishop and on all who have benefices.

7. The seminary is to be under the jurisdiction of the Bishop, the dean of the cathedral church, and the dean of the cathedral chapter.

8. The ordinary will diligently examine all that are to teach in the seminary.

9. Those disobeying this decree are excommunicated, and cannot teach for three years.[13]

The recognition of the disadvantages of the University system as a medium of clerical training had resulted in a widespread dissatisfaction and a definite trend toward the rehabilitation of the ancient cathedral and episcopal schools. There was a feeling, however, that the simple restoration of these would not be sufficient,[14]

[13] Mansi, 33, 1029.
[14] A. J. P., I, 672.

and the decree of Cardinal Pole was the first practical expression of the desire for a real and complete reorganization of the system of clerical education.

2.—*The Council of Trent*

The twenty-third session of the Council of Trent, the seventh under Pope Pius IV, was begun on July 15, 1563. The subject for consideration by the Fathers of the Council was the Sacrament of Orders. After the declaration of the dogmatic principles concerning this Sacrament, the question of the reformation of existing conditions pertinent to it was then discussed. The prevalent opinion of ecclesiastics, whether delegates to the Council or not, was that the effective restoration of clerical discipline depended to a great extent on the measures taken for the reform of clerical training and education. Early in the year 1563, the Fathers of the Council had approved the institution of seminaries. A decree ordaining the institution of seminaries, and outlining in detail the organization of such institutions, was drafted and presented to the Council during the course of this session. It is contained in the 18th chapter of the decrees of the twenty-third session concerning reformation. The full text of the decree is as follows:

Introduction

> Whereas the age of youth, unless it be rightly trained, is prone to pursue the pleasures of the world; and unless it be formed, from its tender years, unto piety and religion, before habits of vice have wholly taken possession of men, it never will perfectly, and without the greatest and almost singular help of Almighty God, persevere in ecclesiastical discipline, the holy synod ordains that all cathedral, metropolitan, and other churches greater than these, shall be found, each according to the measure of its means and the extent of its diocese, to maintain, to educate religiously, and to instruct in ecclesiastical discipline, a certain number of youths of their city or diocese; or if that number cannot there be found, of that province, in a college to be chosen by the Bishop for this purpose near the said churches, or in some other convenient place.

Students

> And into this college shall be received such as are at least

twelve years old, born in lawful wedlock, and who know how to read and write competently, and whose disposition and inclination afford a hope that they will always serve in the ecclesiastical ministry. And it wishes that the children of the poor be principally selected; though it does not, however, exclude those of the more wealthy, provided they be maintained at their own expense, and carry before them a desire of serving God and the Church. The Bishop, having divided these youths into as many classes as shall seem fit to him, according to their number, age, and progress in ecclesiastical discipline, shall, when it seems convenient to him, assign some of them to the ministry of the churches, and keep the others in the college to be instructed; and shall supply the place of those who have been withdrawn by others; so that this college may be a perpetual seminary of the ministers of God.

Internal Rule

And to the end that the youths may be more conveniently trained in the aforesaid ecclesiastical discipline, they shall always at once wear the tonsure and the clerical dress; they shall learn grammar, singing, ecclesiastical computation, and the other liberal arts; they shall be instructed in Sacred Scripture, ecclesiastical books, the homilies of the saints; the manner of administrating the Sacraments, especially those which shall seem united unto hearing confessions; and the forms of the rites and ceremonies. The Bishop shall take care that they be every day present at the Sacrifice of the Mass, and that they confess their sins at least once a month, and receive the Body of their Lord Jesus Christ according to the judgment of their confessors; and on feast days serve in the cathedral and other churches of the place.

General Administration

All which, and other things advantageous and needful unto this object, all Bishops shall ordain, with the advice of two of the senior and most discreet canons whom themselves have chosen, as the Holy Spirit shall have directed; and shall make it their care, by frequent visitation, that the same be always observed. The forward and incorrigible, and the disseminators of evil morals, they shall punish sharply, even, if necessary, by expulsion; and removing all hindrances, they shall carefully attend to whatsoever things appear to tend to preserve and advance so pious and holy an institution. And inasmuch as some certain revenues will be necessary for raising the fabric of the college, and for paying their salaries to the teachers and servants, and for maintaining the youths and for other expenses; besides those funds which are, in some churches and places, set aside for instructing or maintaining youths, and which are hereby to be looked upon as applied to this seminary under the said charge of the Bishop; the same Bishops, with the advice of two of the chapter, of whom one shall be chosen by the Bishop, and the other by the chapter itself, and also of two of the clergy of the city, the election of one of whom shall in like manner appertain to the Bishop, and of the Bishop, and of the other to the clergy,

Maintenance

shall take away a portion of the entire fruits of the episcopal income, and of the chapter, and of all dignities soever, prebend, offices, personates, portions, abbeys, and priories, of what order soever, even though regular, or of what quality or condition soever, they be, and of hospitals which are conferred under title or administration, according to the constitution of the Council of Vienne, which begins *Quia Contingit;* and of all benefices soever, even those belonging to regulars, even if they be under any right of patronage, even if they be exempted, even if they be of no diocese, or are annexed to other churches, monasteries, hospitals, or to any other pious places, even such as are exempted; as also of the fabrics of churches, and of other places, and likewise of all other ecclesiastical revenues or proceeds soever, even those of other colleges; in which, however, there are not actually seminaries of scholars, or of teachers, for promoting the common good of the church; for the synod wills that such places be exempted, except in regard of such revenues as may remain superfluous over and above the fitting support of said seminaries; or of bodies, or confraternities, which in some places are called schools, and of all monasteries, with the exception of the mendicants; also of the tithes appertaining in any way to laymen, out of which ecclesiastical subsidies are wont to be paid, and to the soldiers of any military body, or order, the brethren of Saint John of Jerusalem alone excepted; and they shall apply to, and incorporate with, the said college that portion so deducted, as also certain simple benefices, of what quality and dignity soever they be, or even prestimonies or prestimonial portions, as they are called, even before they fall vacant, without prejudice to the divine service, or to those who hold them. And this shall have effect, even if the benefices be reserved or appropriated; nor shall these unions and applications of the said benefices be suspended, or in any way hindered, by the resignation thereof, but shall still in any case have effect, any way in which they may be vacated, even if it be in the Roman court, and any constitution whatsoever notwithstanding.

And they shall be compelled by the Bishop of the place, by ecclesiastical censures and other legal remedies, even by calling in for this purpose, if it shall seem fit, the secular arm, to pay this portion of benefices, dignities, personates, and of all and each the above named revenues, not merely on their own account, but also on account of what pensions soever they may chance to have to pay to others, out of the said revenues or fruits, keeping back, however, a sum equivalent to what they have to pay on account of said pensions; any privileges as regards all and singular the above-mentioned premises, exemptions, even such as might require a special derogation, any custom, even immemorial, or any appeal and allegation which might hinder the execution hereof, notwithstanding. But in case it should happen that, by means of the said unions obtaining their effect, or from some other cause, the said seminary should be found to be wholly or in part endowed, then shall the portion deducted as above from all benefices, and incorporated by the Bishop, be remitted, either wholly or in part, as the actual circumstances shall require. But if the prelates of cathedral and other greater churches should be negligent in erecting the said seminary, and in preserving the same, and should refuse to pay their share, it will be the duty of the Archbishop sharply to rebuke the Bishop, and to compel him to comply with all the matters aforesaid, and of the provincial synod (to rebuke and compel in like manner) the Archbishop, and earnestly to take care that this holy and pious work be, wherever possible, as soon as possible, proceeded with. But the Bishop shall annually receive the accounts of the revenues of the said seminary, two deputies from the chapter, and the same number deputed from the clergy of the city, being present.

Professors

Furthermore, in order that provision may be made for the teaching in schools of this nature at less expense, the holy synod ordains that Bishops, Archbishops, Primates, and other Ordinaries of places, shall constrain and compel, even by the subtraction of their fruits, those who possess any professorships of theology, and others to whom is attached the office of lecturing or teaching, to teach those who are to be educated in said schools, personally, if they be competent, otherwise by competent substitutes chosen by the same professors, and to be approved of by the Ordinary. And if, in the judgment of the Bishop, they be not fit, they shall nominate another who is fit, all power of appeal being set aside. But should they neglect this, the Bishop himself shall depute one. And the aforesaid (masters) shall teach those things which shall seem expedient to the Bishop. And henceforth, those offices or dignities which are called professorships of theology, shall not be conferred on any but doctors, or masters, or licentiates in sacred letters or canon law, or on other competent persons, and such as can personally discharge that office; and any provisions made otherwise shall be null and void; all privileges and customs soever, even though immemorial, notwithstanding.

Exceptions

But if the churches in any province labor under so great poverty that in some of them a college cannot be erected, the provincial synod, or the metropolitan with the two oldest suffragans, shall take care to erect one or more colleges, as shall be judged convenient, in the metropolitan church, or in some other more convenient church of the province, out of the revenues of two or more churches, in which singly a college cannot be conveniently established, where the youths of those churches shall be educated. But in churches which possess ample dioceses, the Bishop shall have one or more seminaries in his diocese, as shall seem expedient to him, which shall, however, be entirely dependent in all things on the one erected and established in the episcopal city.

Conclusion

Lastly, if either upon the occasion of the said unions, or the taxation, or assignment and incorporation of the said portions, or from some other cause, any difficulty should happen to arise by reason of which the institution, or maintenance of the said seminary may be hindered or disturbed, the Bishop, with the deputies as above, or the provincial synod, according to the customs of the country, shall have power, according to the character of the churches and benefices, to regulate and order all and each the matters which shall seem necessary and expedient for the advancement of the said seminary, even so as to modify or enlarge them, if need be.[15]

This decree contains the primary institution of diocesan and provincial seminaries properly so called, and marks the beginning of a new era in clerical education. In a letter to the legates then presiding over the Council, St. Charles Borromeo conveyed the approval of the Holy Father, Pius IV, [16] who praised the decree as a result of Divine inspiration.[17] The delegates to the Council themselves felt that this great achievement alone would be more than sufficient to compensate them for their labors during the lengthy conciliar sessions.[18]

The legal and practical value of the decree has been demonstrated by its permanent stability, since it has always remained the foundation of all subsequent legislation on clerical education, including that contained in the New Code of Canon Law. Its provisions eventually produced their desired effect, even though many Bishops failed to comply with them immediately, or to the fullest extent.

3.—*The Immediate Post-Tridentine Period*

The Councils of the latter half of the sixteenth century almost invariably devoted a special section of their canons to the subject

[15] Buckley, *Canons and Decrees of the Council of Trent*, pp. 171-74; Pallavincio, *Istoria del Concilio di Trento*, XXI, c. 12, n. 17.
[16] Pallavicino, *Istoria del Concilio di Trento*, XXII, c. 1, n. 14.
[17] Pallavicino, *op. cit.*, XXIV, c. 9, n. 6.
[18] Pallavicino, *op. cit.*, XXI, c. 8, n. 3.

of seminaries. Most of them merely reiterated briefly the provisions of the Council of Trent, and demanded the erection of a seminary within a specified period, ranging from three to six months.[19] Further means to provide funds for their erection are often suggested, such as the solicitation of donations from the rich, but usually nothing was mentioned beyond the content of the Tridentine decree. The legislation promulgated for the Milanese Church, however, was an exception to the general rule, and renders this period most important in the history of clerical education. Up to the year 1570, the Archbishop of Milan, St. Charles Borromeo, had founded several seminaries, both major and minor, in his diocese.[20] The regulations for the government and administration of these institutions were formulated by the Cardinal in his famous "*Institutiones Seminarii*," [21] which constitute the greatest juridic development on the subject of seminaries since the Tridentine decree. They are recognized as the best interpretation of the mind of Trent with regard to seminaries, and contained the sanctioned norms for their administration.[22] The celerity with which the saintly Cardinal put into practical operation the provisions of Trent, and his general zeal and activity in the cause of clerical education, have won for him the well merited title of "*Patron of Seminaries.*" [23] It will be necessary here to consider briefly the general schema of the *Institutiones*. It would be impossible to discuss it in detail, since it contains complete and minute regulations for seminary discipline.

A definite distinction was made between a major seminary for the study of philosophy and theology, and a minor seminary for the study of humanities.[24] Although this division had some precedent before the Council of Trent, the latter did not apply it specifically to seminaries. The *Institutiones* were divided into three general

[19] Council of Rouen (1581)—Harduin, 10, 1256; Council of Rheims (1583)—Harduin, 10, 1290; Council of Mechlin (1570), c. 1—Harduin, 10, 1199; Council of Tours (1583), c. 21—Harduin, 10, 1437; Council of Toulouse (1590), c. 5—Harduin, 10, 1811; Council of Aquila (1596), c. 12—Harduin, 10, 1904.

[20] Giussano, *Life of St. Charles Borromeo*, I, 106.

[21] *Acta Ecclesiae Mediolanensis*, II, 859-78.

[22] "Qui concinnandis seminarii constitutionibus manum apponit, rectissimas sanctissimasque normas mutuari poterit a S. Carolo . . . , si praesertim Patrum Tridentinorum menti velit inhaerere . . . ," Lucidi, *De Visitatione*, II, 335, n. 9.

[23] Benedict XIV, *Institutiones Ecclésiasticae*, II, 223; Benedict XV, Motu Proprio "*Seminaria clericorum*," Nov. 4, 1915—Fontes, n. 708.

[24] *Acta Ecclesiae Mediolanensis*, II, 866.

sections. The first part contained general regulations for administration. Starting with the return of the student from summer vacation, the opening exercise of the year was a week's retreat. The first chapter then proceeds to outline the requirements necessary for the spiritual advancement of the students. The second chapter deals with the curriculum of studies, and the following two chapters treat of the necessity of homiletics and the study of plain chant. Chapter five contains the regulations for temporal administration, and the next chapter of the section outlines the horarium for the entire year. The section concludes with general directions for vacation time.

The second part deals with the constitution of officials deemed necessary for administration. The immediate supervision of the seminary was placed in the hands of a Rector, who was to be aided by the following officials: a Vice-Rector, Confessor or Spiritual Director, Prefect of Studies, Professors, and a Treasurer. Provision was also made for minor officials, such as a Procurator, who was to do all the actual buying, and a bookkeeper; and even for servants, such as cooks, bakers, and others. A chapter is devoted to each of these officials, and a detailed description of their duties given. The concluding portion of the *Institutiones* delineates means to promote the spiritual and temporal welfare of the students, and comprises regulations for spiritual exercises; for discipline in general; for dress, study, recreation, and the care of the sick among the community. The supreme jurisdiction of the Bishop is indicated throughout the entire document. A formula is given for his official visitation to the seminary, and provision is made for a monthly meeting of the deputies and the Rector in his presence.

CHAPTER FOUR

The fundamental legislation relative to the constitution, methods, and government of ecclesiastical seminaries has remained unchanged for the past three centuries.[1] This is evident from a comparative analysis of the Tridentine decree and the legislation contained in the New Code of Canon Law. In both documents the jurisdiction of the seminary is a prerogative of the Bishop. The two commissions instituted by the Council of Trent are perpetuated by the Code, although substantial changes appear in their personnel and tenure of office. The system of internal administration sanctioned by the Code is the same as that outlined by St. Charles Borromeo. Since the scope of this dissertation embraces only these phases of seminary administration, much of the legislation relative to them, including especially many decisions of the Congregations, will be discussed in the commentary on the canons of the Code, according to the provisions of canon 6, numbers 2 and 3. A consideration of the important legal developments between the Council of Trent and the New Code, not directly pertinent and necessary to the understanding of the Code legislation, will conclude the juridic history of seminaries.

1.—*Episcopal Jurisdiction*

The entire content of the Tridentine decree indicates the plenitude of episcopal jurisdiction over diocesan seminaries. With regard to spiritual administration it states, "All which, and other things advantageous and needful unto this end, all Bishops shall ordain . . . and shall make it their care . . . that the same be always observed." For temporal administration it further provides that ". . . the Bishop . . . shall have power . . . to regulate and order all and each matters which shall seem necessary and expedient for the advancement of the said seminary, even so as to modify and enlarge them, if need be." The extent of episcopal power became evident through subsequent conciliar decrees given in response to the many questions which

[1] Preface to Motu Proprio of Benedict XV., "*Seminaria clericorum,*" in A. E. R., LIV, 130.

inevitably arose concerning it. These matters were first referred simply to the Congregation of the Council. Pope Benedict XIII, however, prompted by the failure of Bishops to comply with the decree of the Council of Trent, instituted a Congregation of Seminaries in the Papal constitution "*Creditae Nobis,*" May 9, 1725.[2] The Congregation was to be composed of members of the Congregation of Bishops and Regulars, and of the Congregation of the Council. The Secretary of the latter Congregation became ex-officio the Secretary of the new body. The personnel of the Congregation was therefore restricted to members of these two older Congregations. This exercise of cumulative jurisdiction is apparent from the fact that decrees relative to seminary matters are found in the various Collectanea of both Congregations. The decree implied that the chief purpose of the Congregation was to ensure the erection of diocesan seminaries and to regulate financial matters, although it undoubtedly extended its activities to all phases of seminary administration.[3]

Pope Leo XII expressly exempted seminaries from the jurisdiction of the Congregation of Studies.[4] With the reform of the Roman Curia by Pope Pius X, seminaries were placed under the Congregation of the Consistory.[5] Pope Benedict XV then issued his Motu Proprio, "Seminaria clericorum," November 4, 1915,[6] by which the present Congregation of Seminaries and Universities was instituted. The office of the former Congregation of Studies was assimilated to the new Congregation. The Cardinal Prefect is ipso facto a member of the Congregation of the Consistory, and the Secretary is to be numbered among its Consultors. The Cardinal Secretary of the latter Congregation, together with the Assessor, are likewise members ex-officio of the Congregation of Seminaries. The latter, by means of which the general principle of Papal supervision of clerical discipline is maintained with regard to seminaries, has been perpetuated by the New Code.[7]

The Council of Trent, while vesting the Bishop with immediate jurisdiction over the seminary, wisely provided for two advisory com-

[2] Fontes, I, 288, n. 7.
[3] Pope Pius X, Const. "*Sapienti consilio*" (1908)—A. A. S., I, 7.
[4] A. J. P., II, 1778.
[5] Const. "Sapienti Consilio," loc. cit.
[6] Fontes, n. 708.
[7] Canon 256.

missions. A Bishop is necessarily occupied with many important diocesan affairs, and hence cannot give personal and constant attention to the direction of the seminary. The institution of the commissions was intended to obviate the danger of error on the part of the Bishop in arriving at a satisfactory solution of problems of administration, and in the adoption of policies relative to it.[8] The Bishop had the right to select the two canons who were to compose the commission of general administration, and also two of the members of the commission on economic administration. The clergy of the city were to elect one of the members of the latter, but if they failed to name a representative within a stated time, or were negligent in their election, the Bishop himself could name him.[9] In the event that no cathedral chapter existed in the diocese, the Congregation of the Council decided that the Bishop should select two of the older and more experienced of the diocesan priests to serve on the commission of economic administration.[10] The appointment of the commissions did not derogate in any way from the rights of the Bishop in seminary administration. They merely acted in an advisory capacity, and had only a consultative vote.[11] Nevertheless, their advice had to be sought on matters within their respective competence, and without it the Bishop could not act validly.[12] There was, however, no obligation to follow the advice given, and the Bishop could either act upon it or reject it according to his own prudent judgment.[13] Pope Benedict XIV, in the constitution "*Ad militantis,*" March 30, 1742, decreed that there should be no suspensive appeal from the decision of the Bishop in these matters.[14]

The absolute jurisdiction accorded to Bishops is evident from many other decrees, most of which, however, pertain to the commentary

---

[8] Wernz, *Jus Decretalium*, III, n. 94.

[9] S. C. C. in Feretrana, Dec. 6, 1648—Pallotini, v. *seminarium*, §II, n. 11.

[10] S. C. C. in Pinhelen, Jan. 15, 1791—Thes. S. C. C., LX, 11; A. S. S., I, 696.

[11] S. C. C. in Lucana, Nov. 19, 1616—Ferraris, *Bibliotheca*, v. seminarium, n. 108; Wernz, *Jus Decretalium*, III, n. 94; A. J. P., I, 675; Pignatelli, *Consultationes Canonicae*, cons. 81, nn. 79, 194; Barbosa, Comm. in Conc. Trid., p. 345.

[12] S. C. C. in Aquinaten, Nov. 27, 1852—Pallotini, v. *seminarium*, §IV, nn. 2, 3, 4; A. S. S. I, 694; Wernz, *Jus Decretalium*, III, n. 94; Bouix, *De Episcopo*, II, 72; Barbosa, *De Officio et Potestate Episcopi*, alleg. 77, n. 33; Pignatelli, *op. cit.*, cons. 81, n. 194; Frances, *De Ecclesiis Cathedralibus*, p. 506.

[13] Barbosa, *Comm. in Conc. Trid.*, p. 345; also the citations under note 12.

[14] Fontes, n. 326, n. 34; Pallotini, v. *seminarium* §II, 21, 32.

on the Code, and will be mentioned in their proper place. The most important restriction placed upon it was relative to the transfer of the administration of diocesan seminaries to religious orders. This was considered too great a derogation from the Tridentine law to be within episcopal competence. The first definite legislation appeared in 1722, when the Bishop of Concepcion, Central America, asked permission of the Holy See to transfer his seminary to the Jesuits.[15] The request implied that it was customary to ask such permission, which was granted under the conditions that the students should be named by the Bishop, and that the seminary should remain "..*Sub patrocinio, protectione, et subjectione episcopi.*" Prior to this, in 1714, a case had been presented to the Congregation of the Council in which the seminary had already been transferred to a religious congregation, but no mention is made of securing permission of the Holy See.[16] After the year 1722 many such requests are found,[17] although no definite decision concerning the necessity of securing permission had been given. Nevertheless, it was implied by the constant discipline of the Congregation of the Council, in whom the legitimate authorty for granting the faculty was vested.[18] For example, when it was learned that a seminary had been transferred to a religious order, the Congregation immediately inquired of the Bishop whether he had the required permission, or whether at least the provisions of Trent had been safeguarded.[19]

It was the middle of the nineteenth century before the law was definitely formulated by the Congregation of Bishops and Regulars. In a section dealing with the method of the Congregation in granting approbation to new institutes of simple vows, Bizzari[20] mentions certain observations made in approving the constitutions of the Mission Congregation of St. Francis de Sales. Among them is the following: "*Non possunt episcopi concredere directionem seminariorum Ordinibus regularibus aliisque institutis sine venia Apos-*

---

[15] Thes. S. C. C., II, 191; Benedict XIV, *De Synodo,* V, c. 11, n. 9.

[16] Lucidi, *De Visitatione,* II, c. VI, n. 38.

[17] S. C. C. in Albanen, June 23, 1742—Zamboni v. *seminarium,* §III, n. 14; Bouix, *De Episcopo,* II, 73.

[18] ". . . seminaria quae legitima auctoritate tradita sunt curae et regimini alicujus ordinis regularis; legitima auctoritate; i.e., Sacre Congregaitonis Concilii interpretis."—Ferraris, *Bibliotheca,* v. seminarium, nn. 198-99; A. S. S. II, 54.

[19] S. C. EE. et RR., Sept. 3, 1864, A. S. S., III, 54.

[20] Collectanea EE. et RR., p. 797.

tolicae Sedis." This legislation was restated even more explicitly by the same Congregation in 1861, and was enforced even though an institute was approved especially for the work of clerical education. The Congregation of Bishops and Regulars, in a decree re-establishing the Society of the Oratory in France, March 22, 1864, gave it the privilege of accepting the government of minor seminaries for a period of ten years without recourse to the Holy See.[21] If a Bishop sought to place a major seminary under their direction, permission had to be asked in every single case. The ten year privilege, which carried with it the right of administration without the intervention of the deputies, was also enjoyed by the Eudists,[22] and by the Sulpicians.[23] The latter received the privilege in perpetuity from Pope Benedict XV.[24]

2.—*The Commissions of Administration*

The Council of Trent instituted two commissions—the first one for general administration, consisting of two canons selected by the Bishop; the second for the administration of temporal affairs, composed of two canons, one selected by the chapter, the other by the Bishop; and two of the diocesan clergy, one elected by the clergy, the other selected by the Bishop. Some canonists were of the opinion that besides these, a third had been constituted by the Council for the purpose of receiving the annual report. Bouix,[25] Ferraris,[26] Maupied, and Craisson,[27] in advancing this theory, base their argument on the fact that the Council of Trent stated that the report should be received by the Bishop in the presence of two deputies from the chapter, and a like number from the clergy, and contend that these deputies were intended by the Council to be chosen by the bodies whose representatives they were to be. This would exclude the members of the first commission, both of whom were chosen by the Bishop, and the members of the second also, since two of its members were also chosen by him. Vecchiotti [28] adhered to this

[21] A. J. P., VII, 763.
[22] Feb. 19, 1864—A. J. P., IX, 510.
[23] A. J. P., IX, 510.
[24] Dec. 20, 1921—A. A. S., XIV (1922), 37.
[25] *De Episcopo*, II, 72; *De Capitulis*, p. 424.
[26] *Bibliotheca*, v. seminarium, n. 9.
[27] Cf. N. R. T., V (1873), 630.
[28] *Institutiones Canonicae*, II, 179.

opinion also, but stated that the practice of the Congregation of the Council was to consider the second and third commissions identical. The opposite view was held by many reputable canonists,[29] who were upheld by a decision of the Congregation of the Council, March 31, 1855,[30] which declared the commission to receive the annual report identical with that constituted by Trent for temporal administration. Hence the following appeared in the statutes of the diocese of Malines:[31] "Quattuor deputati pro temporalibus, electi juxta legem Tridentinam, similiter votum emittent consultativum in omnibus quae respiciunt totius seminarii administrationem temporalem, sub qua comprehenditur annua redditio computuum . . ."

The Bishop was not bound to ask the advice of the chapter or of the clergy in selecting the members from among their number whom the common law gave him the right to choose.[32] The election of its representative by the chapter was usually done by means of a scrutinium or poll of the votes of the members, a majority of which decided the election,[33] according to the usual rules for chapter elections.[34] With regard to the election of the representatives of the diocesan clergy, there were many controverted points. Ferraris[35] contended that the election should take place in a diocesan synod, or at least in some formal convention of the city clergy, in accordance with the general principle that nominations and elections by a corporate body should be done in a legitimate convocation of the members thereof.[36] While this appears to have been the usual procedure,[37] Corradus[38] denied that it could be urged for the validity of the election, since the Council of Trent had made no stipulation

[29] Pallottini, v. *seminarium*, §4, n. 1; Pignatelli, *Consultationes Canonicae*, cons. 81, n. 11; Barbosa, *De Officio et Potestate Episcopi*, alleg. 93, n. 22; Van Espen, *Jus Ecclesiasticum*, II, I, tit. II, c. 2.

[30] S. C. C. in Oristan, *Thes.* S. C. C., CXIV, 125; A. S. S., I, 692; A. J. P., VII, 871; A. J. P., IX, 630.

[31] N. R. T., V (1873), 630.

[32] S. C. C. in Arminen (1607)—Pallottini, v. *seminarium*, §2, n. 12.

[33] S. C. C. in Tudertina, Sept. 15, 1792—*Thes.* S. C. C. LXI, 160; A. J. P., IX, 627.

[34] Barbosa, *De Canonicis*, XXXVIII, n. 1.

[35] *Supplementum*, v. seminarium, p. 720.

[36] S. C. EE. et RR. in Luganen. (1893)—*Anal. Ecc.*, I, 13.

[37] S. C. C. in Tudertina, Sept. 15, 1792—Thes. S. C. C. LXI, 160; Pignatelli, *Consultationes Canonicae*, X, cons. 23, n. 2; Van Espen, *Jus Ecclesiasticum Universum*, II, II, c. 3, n. 12.

[38] *Praxis Beneficiaria*, IV, c. 8, n. 28.

to that effect. In any case, a viva voce election was valid.[39] The right to participate in the election of the representative of the clergy was also a disputed point.[40] Bouix [41] and other canonists [42] held that all the diocesan clergy, both within and outside the cathedral city, had the right to vote in the election. Their theory was based on the fact that the administration of the seminary was a matter affecting the entire diocese, and the restriction of the right of election to the urban clergy, to the exclusion of all others, was unfair and in reality defeated the purpose of the law. In a case presented to the Congregation of the Council [43] the following arguments in support of this opinion were favorably considered: namely, that the Tridentine law makes no distinction; that the entire clergy are subject to tax; and that even though the representative be chosen from the city, there is nothing to prevent the rest of the clergy from participating in the election. Some canonists, however, such as Benedict XIV [44] and Giraldi,[45] held that the right to elect belonged to the clergy of the city alone, since the Tridentine decree stated "..duorum de clero civitatis." Two decisions of the Congregation of the Council imply that the former opinion is correct, inasmuch as they not only seem to presuppose that the Vicars Foreane have the right to participate in the election, but by virtue of particular circumstances grant the right to the latter to act as delegates for the rest of the diocesan clergy.[46] A decision of July 15, 1893, forbade the members of the Society of the Oratory to participate in these elections, even though they are considered as secular priests.[47] Another decision denied this right to the members of the cathedral chapter.[48] In the case of the absence or temporary disability of one of the deputies, the right to choose a substitute did not belong necessarily to the Bishop, but to the body who had originally elected the representative.[49]

---

[39] S. C. C. in Tudertina, Sept. 15, 1792—*Thes.* S. C. C. 61, 160; A. J. P. IX, 627.

[40] N. R. T., V (1873), 356, footnote 1.

[41] *De Capitulis*, p. 481.

[42] Corradus, *op. cit.*, IV, c. 8, n. 28; Pallottini, v. *seminarium*, §2, n. 10; Van Espen, *Jus Ecclesiasticum Universum*, II, II, c. 3, n. 12.

[43] S. C. C. in Luganen. Jan. 28, 1893—*Anal. Ecc.*, I, 13.

[44] *De Synodo Diocesana*, V, c. 11, n. 3.

[45] *Espositio Juris Pontificii*, II, 984.

[46] S. C. C. in Buscoducen. Jan. 21, 1879—*Anal. Ecc.*, I, 13; A. S. S., XXV, 623; S. C. C. in Luganen. Jan. 28, 1893—*Anal. Eccl.*, *loc. cit.*

[47] S. C. C. in Auximana, A. S. S. XXVI, 174; *Anal. Eccl.*, I, 354.

[48] S. C. C. in Maceraten, Aug. 17, 1901—A. S. S., XXXIV, 180.

[49] S. C. C. in Arboren., March 31, 1855—A. S. S., I, 696.

Two important developments relative to the personnel of the commissions occurred in the latter half of the nineteenth century. In the United States, the Third Plenary Council of Baltimore inaugurated a radical departure from the Tridentine decree. It stated that for every seminary, whether major or minor, at least *two* deputies should be constituted, one for general administration, and the other for the administration of temporalities. Their selection was to be made by the Bishop after a consultation with the diocesan consultors.[50] On August 27, 1864, the Congregation of Bishops and Regulars issued a decree forbidding directors and members of the seminary faculty to assume positions on the commissions.[51] The Congregation of the Council later reiterated this prohibition.[52] Therefore, while the latter Congregation regarded favorably the selection of the same two canons for both commissions,[53] it reprobated any direct derogation from the decree of Trent. Hence the condition prevalent in France during the last century, namely the appointment of the Superior and Directors of the seminary as sole members of the spiritual commission, and of the Vicar General, the Rector of the Seminary, the Secretary of the Bishop, etc., as members of the temporal commission,[54] could in no wise be sanctioned as a legitimate custom.[55] The view of Bonal,[56] who accorded the force of legitimate custom not only to this, but even to the custom in France of concentrating the administration in the hands of the Bishop alone without any intervention of deputies at all, is inexplicable in view of the previously mentioned decree forbidding derogations in general from the laws of the Council of Trent; in view of the care exercised by the Holy See in the transfer of seminaries to religious; and finally in view of the fact that the Congregation of Bishops and Regulars expressly reprobated such a condition on August 27, 1864, and demanded that the regulations of Trent be observed in their entirety.[57]

The competence of the commissions has not been changed by the Code. The commission of general administration was an advisory

---

50 *Acta et Decreta Conc. Plen. Balt. III*, tit. V, c. 2, n. 179.
51 A. J. P., VII, 868-76; N. R. T., V (1873), 355.
52 S. C. C. in Luganen. Jan. 28, 1893—*Anal. Eccl.*, I, 13.
53 S. C. C. in Buscoducen.—A. J. P. XVIII, 979; Instr. ad. Ordinarios Amer. Meriod., Mar. 15, 1897—Bargilliat, *Monita et Decreta*, p. 29.
54 *Le Canoniste Contemporain*, XI, 324.
55 Pouan, *De Seminario Clericorum*, p. 304.
56 *Institutiones Canonicae*, II, 226.
57 A. J. P., VII, 868.

board in such matters as the formation of seminary regulations, admittance of pupils, selection of teachers, etc.; the commission on economic administration was consulted on the various methods of maintaining the seminary, and on the administration of goods accruing to the institution. Pope Benedict XIV [58] denied the contention of Barbosa [59] and Van Espen [60] that the annual report should be made in synod. He declared that the opinion lacked foundation in either conciliar or pontifical decrees, and that custom alone could justify it. Moreover, the loss of the report after it had been made, or the failure of one of the deputies to ratify it, were not considered sufficient grounds to demand a new report.[61] The opinion of all the deputies had to be asked on matters within their competence, except in the matter of exacting the payment of the stated seminary tax, which pertained only to the Bishop.[62] All the deputies of temporal administration had to be present at the rendition of the annual report, otherwise it was considered invalid.[63] The members of the latter commission were bound to observe the general laws concerning alienations in rendering their advice, and if constituted as actual administrators of the seminary goods, in their mode of action.[64] Thus in 1766 a case was presented to the Holy See in which the Bishop and the members of the administrative commission were guilty of illicit alienation. Faculties were granted through the Congregation of Bishops and Regulars to their various confessors to absolve them from the censures incurred by their act.[65]

According to pre-Code discipline, the members of the two commissions were to hold office perpetually, and could be removed only for a just and legitimate cause,[66] according to the prudent judgment of the Ordinary. A decision of the Congregation of the Council

[58] *De Synodo*, V, c. 11, n. 4.

[59] *De Officio et Potestate Episcopi*, alleg. III, 93, n. 22.

[60] *Jus Ecclesiasticum Universum*, II, II, c. 2, n. 12.

[61] *Thes. S. C. C.*, II, 278; XXXIV, 127; A. J. P., IX, 626

[62] S. C. C., in Nullius, Jan. 19, 1595—A. S. S., I, 693; in Cavrien., Oct. 5, 1594—Zamboni, v. *seminarium*, §3, n. 3; in Tricarien., Mar. 24, 1736—A. S. S., I, 693; Frances, *De Ecclesiis Cathedralibus*, c. XXVIII, n. 504.

[63] Lucidi, *De Visitatione*, II, 360, n. 106; Ojetti, *Synopsis*, 3673.

[64] A. J. P., VIII, 296.

[65] S. C. EE. et RR., in Recanati, March 24, 1766—A. J. P., VIII, 501; XII, 103.

[66] S. C. C., in Compsana (1604)—Pallottini, v. *seminarium*, §2, n. 24; in Sarazinen., A. S. S., I, 695; Bouix, *De Episcopo*, II, 72; Ferraris, *Bibliotheca*, v. seminarium, n. 92; S. C. C. in Salemeten, Jan. 25, 1890—*Thes. S. C. C.*, 149, 68; 61, 160; A. S. S., 22, 597.

mentions excessive expenditures without the consent of the Bishop as a sufficient cause for removal,[67] and Ojetti [68] mentions chronic illness and advanced age. Moreover, when a deputy chosen from the diocesan clergy became a canon he thereby lost his position as deputy.[69]

The selection of chapter members to serve on the commissions inevitably gave rise to questions concerning their right to receive the revenue due to them as members of the chapter during the time in which they were engaged in seminary work. This consisted in the fruits attached to their canonical prebend, and in the daily distributions to canons present either personally or by fiction of law.[70] Barbosa [71] held that canons engaged in study that necessitated their absence from choir should receive the fruits of their prebend, but not the daily distributions. This might be extended to canons appointed for seminary administration or for teaching in the seminary. Frances [72] believed that canons who were connected in any way with seminary administration should have the right even to the daily distributions, in proportion to the time spent in seminary work. Corradus [73] held that those who taught receved the daily stipends distributed in their absence. The Congregation of the Council decided this question with reference to the canons who acted as deputies. Such canons were not to be considered as present in choir by any fiction of law, and lost a third part of the daily distributions in proportion to the days and hours during which they were absent on seminary business.[74] While the decision rendered pertains only to the case as cited, nevertheless none of the elements found in it are otherwise than would probably be verified in any case of dispute concerning the cumulative office of canons and deputies. Nevertheless, Wernz-Vidal [75] warns that the jurisprudence of the Congregation of the Council on this matter was quite variable.

---

[67] S. C. C. in Tudert. Sept. 15, 1792—*Thes.* S. C. C., LXI, 160; A. S. S. I, 696.

[68] *Synopsis*, n. 3673.

[69] S. C. C., in Aquen., Jan. 23, 1873—A. J. P., XIV, 381.

[70] Ojetti, *Synopsis*, n. 1840.

[71] *De Canonicis*, n. 10, p. 155.

[72] *De Ecclesiis Cathedralibus*, c. XXVIII, n. 277.

[73] *Praxis Beneficiaria*, I, 58, c. 1, n. 11.

[74] S. C. C., in Anagni, Nov. 20, 1819—*Thes.* S. C. C., LXXIX, 326.

[75] *De Personis*, III, n. 690.

3.—*Officials of the Seminary*

The object for which seminaries have been instituted, namely the spiritual formation of the students, and their training in science and discipline, necessitated administrative regulations for the government of the seminary, and the instituton of moderators to ensure their observance. The Council of Trent placed the administrative supervision in the hands of the Bishop, and mentions only the commissions instituted to advise him, and the teachers. The proper functioning of the seminary system, however, required a more complex internal organization, and the recognition of this need prompted St. Charles Borromeo to institute a complete system of seminary discipline, routine, and administration. This system has been used generally since the sixteenth century, and is the foundation of the organization sanctioned by the Code.

According to the provisions of St. Charles, the chief moderators were the Rector, Vice-Rector, Spiritual Director or Confessor, Professors, and an Econome or Treasurer.[76] The Rector was the immediate superior and all the other officials were subordinate to him. This fundamental concept prevailed down to the formation of the Code, although in some places the direction of the Seminary was not placed in the hands of a Rector, but was controlled by the professors as a corporate body.[77] All officials were to be named by the Bishop, after a consultation with the commission for general administration.[78] The office of the moderators and professors, unlike that of the deputies, was not considered perpetual, and the Bishop could remove them whenever he deemed it advisable.[79]

The most important legal question relative to the rights of seminary rectors before the Code was that of parochial jurisdiction. The Council of Trent had decreed that parish priests should have jurisdiction over the territory within their parochial boundaries. From them alone could the faithful of the parish receive the Sacraments, and they had exclusive competence in all things pertaining to

---

[76] *Acta Ecclesiae Mediolanensis*, II, 867.

[77] Vieban, art. "*seminary*," Catholic Encyclopedia, XIII, 695-702.

[78] S. C. C. in Fundana (1869)—Pallottini, v. *seminarium*, §2, n. 18; Lucidi, *De Visitatione*, II, 346, n. 33.

[79] S. C. C. in Tricarien, Mar. 24, 1735—*Thes. S. C. C.*, VII, 193; in Spoletana, June 22, 1884—Lucidi, *op. cit.*, II, 366, n. 61.

the care of souls.[80] Episcopal jurisdiction over seminaries certainly did not encroach in any way upon the jurisdictional rights already invested in the pastor of the place where the seminary was situated. The institution of a seminary rector, however, cast some doubt upon the further right of the pastor of the place to exercise parochial jurisdiction over the students and attaches of the seminary. The exemption of the seminary from the jurisdiction of the proper pastor was considered as a dismembering of the parish,[81] and the Sacred Rota required that the necessity and the utility of the Church demand such a mode of procedure.[82]

Prior to the Code, seminaries were not considered exempt from parochial jurisdiction unless by special indult of the Holy See.[83] Popes Leo XII and Pius VII granted exemptions from parochial jurisdiction in the beginning of the nineteenth century, and it is evident that seminaries were not considered as exempt at that time.[84] This fact is also apparent from the many cases presented to the Congregations concerning this matter. Even when the administration of a seminary had been transferred to a religious order, it was not thereby exempt from parochial jurisdiction,[85] for the privileges of the order were not communicated to the seminarians, who remained subject to the authority of the Bishop. Very often, however, such exemption privileges were granted to the religious orders,[86] and they were upheld in individual cases.[87] Between 1860 and 1865 permission was granted to the Marists, Sulpicians, and Oratorians to exercise parochial rights in seminaries under their charge, with the permission of the Ordinary.[88]

The Congregation of Bishops and Regulars, on September 8, 1864, issued a decree in which it was asserted that seminaries, legitimately transferred to the supervision of regulars, were exempt from parochial

---

[80] S. C. Trid. Sess. XXIV, de ref. c. 13, Buckley, *Canons and Decrees of the Council of Trent*, p. 200 ss; Wernz-Vidal, *De Personis*, II, n. 731.

[81] S. C. EE. et RR. in Parmenen. Mar. 13, 1891—A. S. S. XXIV, 59.

[82] S. R. R. Decisiones Recentiores, VII, 134, dec. 68, n. 1; Idem, X, 232, dec. 90, n. 8.

[83] Pouan, *De Seminario Clericorum*, p. 160; Lucidi, *De Visitatione*, II, 352, n. 59; A. J. P., III, 1099.

[84] A. J. P., I, 1110.

[85] A. J. P., VII, 1094.

[86] A. J. P., VII, 1103-06.

[87] S. C. C. in Colimbrien., Mar. 12, 1757—*Thes. S. C. C.*, XXVI, 17.

[88] Lucidi, *De Visitatione*, II, 355, n. 45; A. J. P., II, 1106; Idem, VII, 763-64.

jurisdiction, together with all that lived therein, although provisions must be made to give the pastor of the place a fourth of the funeral stipends.[89] The same Congregation issued a decision on the same subject on March 13, 1891.[90] The Bishop of Berceto, in 1840, had given the sole right of parochial jurisdiction to the Rector of the seminary, in order to secure peace, tranquillity, and the proper maintenance of seminary discipline. His successor gave the jurisdiction back to the pastor of the place. A later episcopal incumbent restored the parochial jurisdiction to the rector of the seminary in 1880. The matter was laid before the Council, which decided that the decree of 1840, bestowing the right of parochial jurisdiction upon the rector of the seminary, should be upheld. This was an implicit sanction of the right of the Bishop, independent of any permission from the Holy See, to exempt the seminary from parochial jurisdiction, and foreshadowed the actual exemption which has been incorporated in the Code.

With regard to the professors, the Council of Trent renewed the provisions of the decree "*Super Specula*" of Honorius III, and stated that teachers of theology should be given a prebend, and that teachers of letters should receive at least the revenue of a simple benefice.[91] The revenues of these prebends or benefices were to accure to them, even though they should be absent.[92] There was a divided opinion among canonists whether the privileges accorded to university professors of theology should be extended to seminary professors.[93] Lucidi [94] and Giraldi [95] contended that only those teaching in more celebrated seminaries should enjoy them. This seems contrary to the provisions of the Council of Trent, which aligned these privileges with the teaching benefices of cathedral churches,[96] and prescribed further that the possessors of such benefices should teach in the seminaries. There seems no reason to believe that the privileges attached to them should cease when those who possessed them began to teach in a seminary. Moreover, in the decree on seminaries, the

---

[89] A. S. S., III, 47.
[90] A. S. S., XXIV, 59-62.
[91] Thomassinus, *Nova et Vetus Disciplina Ecclesiae,* I, II, c. 10, n. 2.
[92] Giraldi, *Expositio Juris Pontificii,* II, 599.
[93] Pouan, *De Seminario Clericorum,* pp. 213-14.
[94] *De Visitatione,* II, 367, n. 64.
[95] *Expositio Juris Pontificii,* II, 601.
[96] Sess. V, *de ref.,* c. 1, Buckley, *Canons and Decrees of the Council of Trent,* p. 25.

Council specifically mentioned the necessity of acquiring funds for the purpose of remunerating the professors.

The Council of Trent states no further requirement for a theological prebend than that the incumbent be competent. Yet Pope Benedict XIV [97] seems to hold that a degree in Canon Law is not sufficient. Other canonists held that a doctorate in Theology is not necessary, and therefore, a doctorate in Canon Law would seem sufficient.[98] Moreover, even though a doctor in Theology or Canon Law should be preferred, the wording of the decree of the Council would render valid the nomination of any person competent to teach. Several decisions were rendered concerning members of the chapter acting as professors in the seminary. A case was presented to the Congregation of the Council in which the Canon Theologian had received a salary from the seminary for his work there as professor, and at the same time had partaken of the daily choral distributions. The decision denied him the right to the latter, and required that a condonation be asked of the Holy See for the distributions he had received.[99] Any of the other canons, when appointed as professor, was considered exempt from choir, but lost the daily distributions, unless actually present.[100] The same held true for a canon appointed as seminary econome.[101]

The obligation of the seminary moderators to discharge the debts incurred by the students was the subject of a case presented to the Congregation of Bishops and Regulars in 1898. The Rector of the Roman Seminary gave permission to a firm of merchants to establish a store in the seminary, and certain students were entrusted with its supervision. After several years, the merchants tried to render the Rector responsible for money that was owed to them, under the provisions of the Italian Civil Code that parents, guardians, etc., are responsible for damages done by those under their charge.[102] The Congregation denied any responsibility on the part of the Rector in the matter.[103] The case was later appealed again by the merchant, but the decision given was the same, with the added provision,

---

97 *De Synodo,* IX, c. 11, n. 16; Idem, *Institutiones Ecclesiasticae,* LVII, n. 5.

98 Bouix, *De Capitulis,* p. 101; Barbosa, *De Potestate et Officio Episcopi,* III, alleg, 55, n. 5; Garzias, *De Beneficiis,* V, c. 4, n. 154; Thes S. C. C. I, 329.

99 S. C. C. in Cathaginien. April 11, 1891—A. S. S., XXIV, 72.

100 S. C. C. in Firmana, May 6, 1843—Thes. S. C. C. C111, 150.

101 Ibidem; A. J. P., IX, 627.

102 *Le Canoniste Contemporain,* XXIV, 373.

103 July 1, 1898—A. S. S., XXXI, 304.

however, that the Cardinal Vicar should investigate the case thoroughly in order to determine the justice of the debt, and to demand restitution from the students concerned.[104]

This brief synopsis of important legal developments relative to the administration of seminaries prior to the Code is a necessary prelude to a commentary on the Code itself. The fact that seminaries were not instituted until the time of the Council of Trent restricts such pertinent legislation to the period from the sixteenth century to the promulgation of the Code in 1918. Nevertheless, the institutes of clerical training which appeared after the first three centuries of the Christian era were progenitors of the Tridentine seminary. The genesis and character of these institutions together with concomitant legislation, constitute an appropriate background for the study of seminary legislation, and a summary discussion of them forms a useful complement for it. The legal provisions cited concerning them are of a very general nature. The majority of the conciliar decrees from the fifth to the tenth century have for their object the erection of clerical schools, but indirectly they manifest the principle of episcopal supervision of such education. From the tenth to the thirteenth century there was a decided trend in the ecclesiastical legislation toward the granting of various privileges to the professors and teachers in the schools and universities. The comparatively few changes made by the New Code of Canon Law in the law regarding seminaries renders a knowledge of the decisions and interpretations cited relative to the Tridentine decree helpful to a proper understanding of the present law.

[104] A. S. S., XXXII, 619.

CHAPTER FIVE

CANONICAL LEGISLATION

Introduction

The legislation in the New Code of Canon Law concerning seminaries is based largely upon the decree of the Council of Trent already cited. In many cases they are both substantially identical, and but few innovations have been introduced. The canons in the title "*De Seminariis,*" therefore, will often be found subject to the interpretative rules stated in the second and third sections of canon six. An analysis of the text and context of these canons will determine whether they incorporate wholly or in part any of the pre-Code legislation, in which case they will be subject either entirely or partially to the interpretation approved prior to the Code. Canon 6, §2 states as a norm for such interpretation the opinion of approved authors, among whom members of the various Congregations are deemed especially reliable and worthy of consideration as prudent and recognized canonists.[1] The term "*auctoritas*" in the second section of canon six a fortiori includes, with reference to the subject under discussion, the various pronouncements of the Pontiffs on the subject of clerical education and seminaries,[2] and the decisions of the Congregations whose competence extended to such matters.[3] The Tridentine legislation on seminaries was first interpreted by the Congregation of the Council, which was later assisted by the Congregation of Bishops and Regulars. The decisions of these Congregations, especially of the former, which held a status relative to the decrees of the Council of Trent similar to that which the Pontifical Commission holds with reference to the New Code, must be considered as authoritative declarations of the meaning of the provisions of the Council. A careful distinction must be preserved, however,

[1] Vermeersch-Creusen, *Epitome,* I, 49; Van Hove, *De Legibus Ecclesiasticis,* p. 69.

[2] *Prümmer, Manuale Juris Canonici,* p. 22.

[3] Michiels, *Normae Generales,* I, 113.

between responses authentically interpreting the law itself, and those which merely apply it to certain peculiar and mutable circumstances.[4]

The canonical discussion of seminary administration will comprise three main aspects: namely, episcopal supervision, the officials, and the two commissions. It must be understood that these phases of administration will be considered only in their relation to diocesan seminaries, with which this section of the Code professedly purports to deal, since inter-diocesan and regional seminaries are governed by special regulations of the Holy See.[5] Matters directly pertaining to the acquisition of finances necessary for the institution and maintenance of the seminary have not been deemed within the scope of this dissertation, and will be treated summarily only insofar as they are necessary for a proper presentation of the legislation on administration. For the same reason, no detailed analysis of the curricula will be given.

Canon 1357.—§1. Episcopi est omnia et singula quae ad rectam Seminarii dioecesani administrationem, regimen, profectum necessaria et opportuna videantur, decernere, eaque ut fideliter observentur, curare, salvis praescriptionibus a Sancta Sede pro casibus peculiaribus latis.

§1.—*Meaning of the Term "Episcopus"*

The legal history of clerical education clearly demonstrates that this phase of ecclesiastical discipline has been under episcopal supervision since the dawn of the Chrstian era. Founded on principles of public law, as outlined in the historical synopsis of legislation pertinent to this question, the sanction of constant practice and of legislative enactments was attached to such supervision centuries before the Council of Trent. It is not surprising, therefore, that the Fathers of the Council placed upon individual Bishops the burden of the erection, conservation, and administration of diocesan seminaries. The first paragraph of canon 1357 is a substantial epitome of antecedent legislation concerning jurisdiction over seminaries. It enunciates the principle not only of the direct and immediate jurisdiction of the Bishops of the place, but further incorporates the equally important principle of the supreme, although indirect, super-

[4] *Periodica*, XVII (1928), pp. 136-38.
[5] Canon 1357 §4.

vision exercised by the Holy See.[6] The right of the Holy See to regulate matters of ecclesiastical discipline for the universal Church certainly includes within its scope questions referring to clerical training and education. Under the Code legislation, the Congregation of Seminaries and Universities has exclusive competence in matters relative to the studies, rule, discipline, and temporal administration of seminaries.[7] The only exception is made for mission countries which come under the jurisdiction of the Congregation for the Propagation of the Faith.[8] In this manner the Holy See has sought to secure stability of clerical education throughout the world. To facilitate its work, the Congregation of Universities and Seminaries ensured the acquisition of recent and correct data concerning the status of individual seminaries by means of a triennial report, which was demanded of each Ordinary in accordance with the provisions of the decree "*Quo uberiore,*" issued by the Congregation on February 2, 1924.[9] The formula for the report was appended to the decree. The triennial period was computed from January 1, 1924. The Ordinaries of France, Italy, Spain, and the adjacent islands rendered their first report in 1924; the remaining Ordinaries of Europe in 1925; and the Ordinaries of America in 1926. The report must be made in Latin. Any change made during the three year period in text-books of Philosophy, Theology, Scripture, or Canon Law, must be reported immediately to the Congregation. This report, however, does not affect in any way the quinquennial report to the Congregation of the Consistory.[10]

Outside of the general supervision by the Congregation of Seminaries, each Bishop is empowered to govern the diocesan seminary according to his own prudent judgment, within, of course, the ambit of the general law. Moreover, his competence in this matter seems to be personal, to the exclusion of the Vicar General. The Tridentine decree uses the term *episcopus* almost exclusively, a usage which has prevailed since that time. The terminology used elsewhere by the Council permits the inference that here the term *episcopus* refers only to the Bishop.[11] The personal solicitude demanded by the

[6] Cocchi, *Commentarium*, VI, 91.
[7] Canon 256 §1.
[8] Canon 252.
[9] A. A. S., XVII (1925), 547 ss.
[10] Canon 340; d'Angelo, *La Curia Diocesana*, pp. 205-06.
[11] E.g. in session XIII, *de ref.*, c. 1, the Council states: "*Episcopi aliique Ordinarii. . . .*"

Council of Trent of the Bishop is required again and again by Conciliar decrees,[12] Congregations, [13] Pontifical documents,[14] and by canonists.[15] The Code itself implies the same personal interest by its exclusive use of the term *Bishop* throughout the title *De Seminariis.*[16] The word *ordinarius* appears in only one instance, namely in canon 1366, §1, and this serves only to emphasize the use of *episcopus* elsewhere throughout the title, for it is used even in the second paragraph of the same canon. Moreover, canon 1357, §2 orders that the Bishop make a personal visitation of the seminary.

This constant emphasis of personal episcopal supervision may have its origin in a desire to obviate unwarranted interference by secular authority,[17] insofar as the Church desires to make clear that the Bishop, her recognized representative, exercises the right which she claims over clerical education. Very probably, however, it originates in the recognition by the Church that such an important diocesan institution should necessarily be an object of the personal solicitude and supervision of the Bishop. Whatever may be its source, it certainly implies the exclusion of the Vicar General from any exercise of jurisdiction over the seminary, unless a special mandate has provided otherwise. Nothing definitely authoritative appeared prior to the Code on the subject of the power of the Vicar General over the diocesan seminary. Canonists [18] stated the same general principle contained in canon 368, §1, which gives the Vicar General powers identical with those of the Bishop, unless restricted either by law

---

[12] Council of Mechlin (1570), c. 2—Harduin, 10, 1199; Council of Toulouse (1590), c. 5—Harduin, 10, 1811; Council of Naples (1699) tit. X, De Seminariis, n. 7—Coll. Lac., I, 229 b; Council of Sienna (1850)—Coll. Lac., IV, 879 d; Third Council of Quebec (1863), c. 6—Coll. Lac., III, 675 a; Acta et Decreta Concilii Plenarii Baltimorensis III, n. 178.

[13] S. C. C. in Ravennatensi—Pignatelli, *Consultationes Canonicae*, IX, cons. 81, n. 51; S. C. EE. et RR., Jan. 18, 1908—Bargilliat, *Monita et Decreta*, 180.

[14] Pius IX, ep. encyc. "*Qui pluribus*," Nov. 9, 1846—Fontes, n. 504; Leo XIII, ep. encyc. "*Etsi nos*," Feb. 15, 1882—Fontes n. 583; Leo XIII, ep. encyc. "*Constanti Hungarorum*," Sept. 2, 1893—Fontes, n. 620; Pius X, ep. encyc. "*E supremi apostolatus*, Oct. 14, 1903—Fontes, n. 653.

[15] Barbosa, *Commentarium in Conc.* Trid., p. 345; "Administratio seminarii est penes ipsum episcopum"—Ojetti, *Synopsis*, n. 3673; Van-Espen, *Jus Ecclesiasticum Universum*, II, I, XI, n. 7; Wernz, *Jus Decretalium*, III, n. 94.

[16] "Codex personalem sollicitudinem pro seminariis ejusque alumnis episcopo inculcat."—Cappello, *Summa Juris Canonici*, II, 387.

[17] Wernz, *Jus Decretalium*, n. 94.

[18] Pichler, *Jus Canonicum*, I, tit. 28, n. 4, p. 93; Barbosa, *De Officio et Potestate Episcopi*, III, alleg. 54, n. 37.

or by the Bishop himself. Cases were cited at length in which the Vicar General could act by special mandate, together with those for which no such permission could be granted; e.g., in the consecration of churches.[19] However, there was no taxative enumeration of cases in which the Vicar General could not act without a special mandate, and a further principle was enunciated, restricting his power also in matters of grave moment.[20] While not mentioned expressly in the former, seminary jurisdiction would seem to be comprised in the latter category.

The possibility of the Vicar General acting in lieu of the Bishop in seminary matters may be deduced from a decision of the Congregation of the Council which grants to the deputies any right to act independent of the Bishop or his Vicar.[21] The decision does not indicate whether such action required any special permission. Several cases may be cited in which such special permission was actually granted. The Council of Aquina, in 1850, placed the direction of the diocesan seminary in the hands of the Bishop, unless the latter specially delegated the Vicar General to act for him in this matter.[22] In 1872 the Archbishop of Malines gave special permission to the Vicar General to act as his representative in affairs pertaining to the seminary.[23] The reservation in these cases, however, may have come from the Bishop as well as from the general law. Pouan [24] is the only available canonist who adverts to this question, and his adherence to the opinion that the Vicar General requires a special mandate to act in seminary matters gives extrinsic probability to the objective arguments already adduced. His words are unequivocal: "Ad Episcopum solum, vel ejus Vicarium Generalem *speciatim ad hoc delegatum*, pertinere . . . administrationem . . . seminarii."

The Code has determined more specifically the cases in which a special mandate is necessary for the Vicar General. Wernz-Vidal [25]

---

[19] Pellegrino, *Praxis Vicariorum*, p. 11; Reiffenstuel, *Jus Canonicum*, I, tit. 24, n. 89.

[20] Wernz-Vidal, *De Personis*, n. 639; Barbosa, *op. cit.*, III, alleg. 54, n. 125; Pellegrino, *op. cit.*, p. 13.

[21] S. C. C. in Ariminen., Feb. 16, 1609—Giraldi, *Exposito Juris Pontificii*, II, 983; Pallotini, v. *seminarium*, §3, n. 31.

[22] Coll. Lac., IV, 998 c.

[23] *Revue des Sciences Ecclesiastiques*, XXVII, 370.

[24] *De Seminario Clericorum*, p. 272.

[25] *De Personis*, n. 639.

mentions those canons in which there is an explicit restriction by the words "..*sine speciali mandato,*" and contends that this is a taxative enumeration, which cannot be extended to similar cases. This seems to be an unwarranted restriction of canon 368. Some canons do not specifically require a special mandate, yet present cases in which the Vicar General cannot act. It is true that such canons are invariably correlated to, or consequences of, some primary canon which requires such a mandate, but in themselves they would include the Vicar General. Therefore the opinion of Prümmer,[26] which is more conservative, seems more logically correct. He holds that the restriction must be made expressly, and this view grants the possibility of both explicit and implicit restrictions. The use of the term *episcopus* would thus constitute an implicit restriction of the power of the Vicar General, even though the necessity of a special mandate were not explicitly stated. This is obvious from an examination of the canons in which the term is used. When the Code desires to express a parity of power between the Bishop and the Vicar General in canons which use the word *episcopus,* it so states in such clauses as, "..*sine Episcopi vel Vicarii Generalis consensu..,*" or their equivalent.[27] Therefore, if the legislators had desired to include the Vicar General in the matter of diocesan seminary jurisdiction, they would have used the term *Ordinarius* or a clause similar to that stated above.

When the Bishop is prevented from performing the duties of his office, the Code empowers the Vicar General to take over the complete supervision of the diocese,[28] including, of course, the seminary. During the vacancy of the episcopal see the right of jurisdiction over the seminary is vested in the chapter, through the Vicar Capitular,[29] in the diocesan consultors, or in an apostolic administrator. The actions of either body must be governed by the axiom, "*Sede vacante, nihil, innovetur,*" and no unnecessary change should be made in

---

[26] *Manuale Juris Canonici,* p. 177.

[27] Canons 327 and 328.

[28] Canon 429 S1, §3.

[29] Canon 429 §3; S. C. C. in Vigilevanen., Jan. 27, 1714—Zamboni, v. *seminarium,* §7, n. 2; Lucidi, *De Visitatione,* II, p. 38f, n. 103; S. C. C. in Oscen., (1585)—Zamboni, v. seminarium, §2, n. 1; A. J. P. IX, 606; S. C.C. in Tricarien., Mar. 24, 1736—*Thes. S. C. C.,* VII, 194.

seminary administration or discipline, nor any change prejudicial to the interests of the new Bishop.[30]

§2.—*Scope of Episcopal Power*

The latitude which this canon gives to the Bishop does not at all mean that he may act with impunity contrary to the general law as stated in the Code. The canon rather grants a scope of action within the limits of the law, according to the prudence and discretion of the Bishop. This may be deduced from the use of the term *administratio*. A distinction might possibly be made between this and *regimen* on the assumption that the former usually refers to the administration of goods, and consequently is here applicable to the temporal administration of seminaries, while the latter comprises regulations for promoting the spiritual and educational progress of the students. However, it seems more correct to consider the two as here practically synonymous. Administration has here a wider meaning than even jurisdiction, and conveys the idea of the Bishop exercising, not a coercive or executive power, but a general supervision of seminary affairs, in order that these may be controlled in accordance with the general laws of the Church. This tenacious adherence to the provisions of the general law was evidenced before the Code in a manifest reluctance to derogate from the Tridentine decree, and by a number of adverse decisions given against Bishops who had acted in contravention of the provisions of Trent for seminaries.[31] The provisions of the Code, therefore, must be the primary norm, and the objective of episcopal regulations should be to secure, in individual cases and under peculiar circumstances, the effect intended by the Code legislation.[32]

New regulations should not be made too hastily, nor should existing statutes be easily changed or abrogated, unless the condition of the times or of the general welfare should obviously demand such

---

[30] Canon 436; Wernz-Vidal, *de Personis*, n. 710; Reiffenstuel, *Jus Canonicum*, III, tit. IX, nn. 13-16; Vermeersch-Creusen, *Epitome*, I, 306.

[31] Ferraris, v. *seminarium*, nn. 32, 41, 43, 44, 45, 61, 64, 65, 66, 82, 98, 123.

[32] ". . . quae (regimen) communi jure canonico primum et deinde peculiaribus regulis ab Episcopo (cui de interno seminarii ordine arbitrium fere omne relictum) cum consilio deputatorum statuendis, gubernatur.", Micheletti, *De Regimine*, p. 272.

changes.[33] Bishops should, therefore, correlate his knowledge of diocesan conditions with a general knowledge of the legislation concerning seminaries, together with its approved interpretation and practical application, and should always have at hand accurate information concerning the status and current condition of the diocesan seminary. For this purpose St. Charles[34] advises that the Chancellor keep in the diocesan archives a folio containing full information concerning the following facts:

1. The document of erection.
2. Any union of benefices made for the seminary.
3. Documents of the Holy See referring to it; e.g., containing privileges, etc.
4. An inventory of its goods and rights.
5. Its constitutions and rules.
6. Reports of the Rector and the Commissions.
7. A list and description of all the officials.
8. A list of the students, together with the following:
    (a) The date of their admission.
    (b) Whether they pay tuition.
    (c) Their names, those of their parents, place of birth, address, parish, and nationality.
    (d) Any sacred orders they may have, together with dimissorial letters, etc.
    (e) A record of their talents and progress in study and morals.

This list, over three centuries old, could well be used now, with the possible change of its second provision to a more general financial report, and with the addition of further information concerning the curriculum.

The administration of a diocesan seminary has a threefold object; first, the moral and religious training of the students; secondly, their

---

[33] ". . . moneri debent episcopi ne de facili novas leges condant, veteraque statuta et ordinationes potestate sibi attributa abrogent, juxta sententiam S. Thomae: Lex non est mutanda quoties experientia quidpiam melius non effert, et in tantum sit bonum ut mala infinita novatio vincat. . . . Quod praecipue observandum est in episcopo successore, qui non facile in hoc a suarum praedecessorum legibus, stylo, modove procedendi discedere debet, eorum gesta contemnens, mutans vel innovans . . . tamen justa praeexistente causa reprehendi non potest qui, exigente tempore rerumque ratione, vel evidentius utilitatis consideratione aliquid ex legibus vel moribus innovat." —Frances, *De Ecclesiis Cathedralibus*, c. 28, nn. 524-40, pp. 524-25.

[34] *Acta Ecclesiae Mediolanensis*, I, 583.

formal education and training in ecclesiastical science and discipline; and lastly, the acquisition and proper administration of finances required for its maintenance.[35] These, of course, presuppose that the seminary has been properly constituted and organized. Canon 1357 §1 empowers the Bishop to decide not only what is necessary, but also what seems to him opportune, to safeguard the welfare and further the progress of the seminary in these matters. After the selection of the most convenient place for the erection of the seminary,[36] his first consideration should be to secure the juridic capacity of the seminary as a moral person, in order that the seminary may, for example, legally acquire, possess and dispose of goods, contract debts, and obtain indults and privileges.[37] This can be accomplished either by a provision of the law itself, or by the formal decree of a legitimate superior.[38] It would seem that the law itself grants juridic personality to the seminary. Canon 99 specifically mentions it as an example of a non-collegiate moral person; canon 1355 permits the levying of a tax for its maintenance; and canon 1356 permits it to receive goods. All these are prerogatives of moral personality.

Gillet [39] contends that, by its very nature, a seminary acquires juridic personality by the fact of its establishment. Before the Code a seminary was considered formally established whenever the students began to live in a community, according to the form prescribed by the Council of Trent.[40] This actual dwelling in community life, the appointment of deputies, and other requirements of Trent, are no longer necessary for legitimate erection according to Cappello,[41] who declares that a formal decree of erection by the Bishop is both sufficient and necessary. Gillet [42] denies, with seeming logic, that such a decree is necessary for the juridic personality of the seminary. He argues that this is one of the cases where such personality is acquired from the law itself, and the Ordinary cannot refuse to recognize it as a prerogative of the seminary once the latter has been legitimately erected. Gillet later admits, however, that the safest

---

[35] De Meester, *Institutiones Juris Canonici*, II, 275.
[36] Canon 1354 § 1; Cappello, *Summa, Juris Canonici*, II, 380.
[37] Cappello, *op. cit.*, I, 195.
[38] Canon 101 § 1.
[39] *La Personallité Juridique en Droit Ecclesiastique*, p. 245.
[40] Garzias, *De Beneficiis*, XII, c. 2, n. 194, p. 373; Ferraris, *Bibliotheca*, v. seminarium, n. 4.
[41] *Op. cit.*, II, pp. 382, 401.
[42] *Op. cit.*, p. 245.

interpretation of canon 100, §1 is that advanced by the Congregation of Religious, November 30, 1922, in a decree concerning juridic personality in institutes of diocesan right.[43] The Congregation states that to obviate any doubt of legitimate personality canon 100, §1 prescribes that moral persons other than the Church and the Holy See be erected by a formal decree. Such a decree need not declare the seminary a moral person in view of the probable opinion that the seminary acquires personality from the Code. However, such a formal decree of erection will obviate any doubt and difficulty as to the exact moment of its legitimate constitution.

D'Angelo[44] mentions several formulae for such a formal decree, of which the following is the briefest:

> "Nos NN. gratia Dei et auctoritate
> Apostolicae Sedis Episcopus N.
>
> Considerantes quam perutile Nostrae diocesi fore novum seminarium ad finem . . . ejusdemque fundationem nunc opportunum in faustis circumstantiis et cum necessariis provisionibus securo futuris; quapropter, praevio assensu tum Nostri consilii pro administratione bonorum ecclesiasticorum Nostrae diocesis, tum Capituli Nostrae Ecclesiae Cathedralis per votum regulariter emisso, Sanctoque Dei nomine invocato, auctoritate Nostra ordinaria, virtute praesentium, erigimus et canonice erectum declaramus nostrum seminarium S. N. in loco N., prout personam moralem ecclesiasticam, ad tramitem sacrorum canonum 99, 100, 101, 102, et 103, cum jure possidendi et bona sua administrandi, sub plena quidem et immediata Nostra jurisdictione in omnibus existentem, ad terminos juris communis ac diocesanorum statutorum probatarumque consuetudinum.
>
> Datum N., sub signo sigilloque Nostris ac nostri cancellarii subscriptione, die . . . mensis . . . anni . . .
> Loc. sig.
>
> N.N. Episcopus N. De mandato Illmi. et Rmi. Episcopi,
> NN. Cancellarius . . .

Although the above decree mentions a previous consultation with the Chapter and the diocesan Commission of financial administration,

[43] A. A. S., XIV (1922), 644.
[44] *La Curia Diocesana*, pp. 157-58.

these cannot be urged as essential either to the constitution or the future direction of the seminary.[45]

It would be impossible to advert to the varied modes of legitimate action to which necessity or opportunity might prompt a Bishop in individual circumstances. He might, for example, find it expedient to amplify the provisions of canon 1367, since it certainly does not contain a taxative enumeration of the exercises necessary for the spiritual welfare of the seminarians; he may vary the requirements and distribution of the curriculum, and the selection of text-books; he may find preferable one or other of the provisions of canon 1355. It may be necessary to restrict or enlarge the number of students to be admitted, since the number should not exceed the needs of the diocese.[46] The selection of the students, or at least the approval of those selected by the Rector, is an inalienable prerogative of the Bishop.[47] He may regulate the service of the seminarians in the Cathedral church,[48] and in general regulate the affairs of the seminary in accordance with his own prudent judgment, as long as he does not act contrary to the general law. Some doubt arose concerning his power to obligate students who were being educated at the expense of the seminary to reimburse the seminary for the expenses incurred, if they left the seminary before their ordination to the priesthood. This was the custom in some dioceses,[49] and was upheld in 1829 by the Congregation of the Council.[50]

The obligation of the Bishop to regulate the reading of periodicals in the seminary has been frequently mentioned by the Holy See. Leo XIII brought the matter to the attention of the Italian Bishops,[51] following a decree which forbade any periodicals unless with the express permission of the Rector, subject to the approval of the Bishop.[52] Pope Pius X, in the Motu Proprio "*Sacrorum Antistitum*," [53] extended this legislation to the entire Church. The reason

[45] S. C. C., June 9, 1855—*Thes. S. C. S.*, CXIV, 198; A. J. P. IX, 630.
[46] S. C. C. in Spoletana, July 11, 1840—Pallotini, v. *seminarium* § 3, n. 9.
[47] S. C. C. in Salernitana, July 10, 1590—Ferraris, *Bibliotheca*, v. seminarium, n. 133; Idem in Auximana., July 1, 1837—Pallotini, v. *seminarium*, § 3, n. 25; in Vigilevanen., Jan. 27, 1714—Pallotini, *loc. cit.*, n. 27.
[48] S. C. C. in Arboren., Sept. 25, 1847—Pallotini, v. *seminarium* § 3, n. 8.
[49] Van-Espen, *Jus Ecclesiasticum Universum*, II, sec. I, tit. XI, c. 1, n. 15; c. 2; n. 6.
[50] In Tiburtina, June 27, 1829—Pallotini, v. *seminarium* § 3, n. 11.
[51] Ep. Encycl., "*Fin dal principio*", Dec. 8, 1902—Fontes, n. 650.
[52] *Jus Pontificium*, VII (1927), p. 26.
[53] Sept. 1, 1910—Fontes, n. 689.

for the prohibition was that such reading would induce an inordinate interest in secular affairs, to the detriment of clerical study and discipline. Canonists disagree as to whether this legislation still retains its legal force.[54] Although no definite decision has been rendered, it is evidently still the desire of the Holy See that Bishops should exercise great care in this matter.[55] Recognized Catholic magazines and periodicals might well be permitted to the students, and even secular magazines of quality and merit, subject to the approval of the seminary authorities and the Bishop. The reading of such magazines could be regulated by placing them in a common reading room, available at stated times. Certainly students should be familiar with the social, economic, and religious conditions and problems of modern life, and it would be extremely unfortunate if they were permitted to be ordained without an adequate concept of the conditions prevalent in the world to which they are to minister.

Whatever the ordinances of the Bishop may be, it is his prerogative to ensure their faithful observance. This may be accomplished in several ways. First of all, they should be incorporated in the approved laws by which the seminary is to be governed.[56] The enforcement of these regulations must then be secured by the appointment of competent officials, who will insist upon and urge their observance.[57] A further means is presented in the frequent visitation prescribed in canon 1357 §2. Moreover, when the regulations of the Bishop are not contrary to the general law, he may impose censures and even privation of office upon those who wilfully and persistently refuse to obey them.[58] Once the seminary regulations have been approved by the Bishop, they should not be changed unless by the Bishop himself, by his successor, or by the Holy See.[59]

§3.—*Restrictions of Episcopal Power*

The final phrase of canon 1357 §1 limits the power of Bishops in those cases where it has been specifically restricted by a decision of

[54] Cappello, *Summa Juris Canonici,* II, 400, footnote 1; Druzbacki, *Jus Pontificium,* VII (1927), 27.

[55] Benedict XV, Ep. to the Belgian Bishops, Feb. 10, 1921—A. A. S., XIII (1921), 127.

[56] Canon 1357 § 3.

[57] Canons 1358 and 1359; Lucidi, *De Visitatione,* II, p. 335, n. 7.

[58] Canon 2331; S. C. C. in Mexicana—Ferraris, *Bibliotheca* v. seminarium, nn. 54 and 102.

[59] Cappello, *Summa Juris Canonici,* II, 388.

the Holy See. This would include decisions of the Congregations,[60] and there seems to be little doubt that the Code intends to include here decisions rendered before 1918, as long, of course, as they are not contrary to the provisions of the Code. The context of the phrase represents a brief but almost verbatim transposition of a section of the Tridentine decree, and while the phrase itself does not appear therein, the principle it enunciates was certainly recognized and implied. Its application is evident in the decisions of the various Congregations. The entire canon, therefore, might be considered as subject to interpretation according to canon 6 §2. If the phrase . . . *salvis praescriptionibus* does not represent an integral incorporation of the law on seminaries, then it at least comes within the provisions of canon 6 §6. Laws promulgated prior to the Code retain their legal force if they are mentioned explicitly or implicitly in it. It would be manifestly impossible to mention explicitly all the decrees of the Holy See concerning seminaries which represent a restriction of episcopal power, but there is here an implicit, though obvious, retention of such provisions. Canon 624 presents an analogous example, which Vermeersch-Creusen cites as containing an explicit mention of certain laws concerning contributions to religious institutes which, because of their number, are nevertheless contained in the Code only implicitly.[61]

Several Pontifical documents support this contention, since they manifest a constant tendency to retain preceding regulations. Pope Pius XI, in a letter to Cardinal Bisleti, August 1, 1922, gave his unqualified approval and confirmation to the prescriptions of his predecessors concerning seminaries.[62] Pope Benedict XV also sanctioned in strong terms the laws promulgated for this purpose by Pope Pius X.[63] The regulations approved by the latter Pontiff for the seminaries of Italy are probably the greatest piece of constructive legislation on seminaries since the Institutes of St. Charles Borromeo, and while they cannot be considered as binding outside of Italy, they at least furnish an excellent directive norm for what the Holy See desires

60 Canon 7.

61 Vermeersch-Creusen, *Epitome,* I, 51.

62 A. A. S., XIV (1922), 449.

63 "Leges pro seminariis tum diocesanis tum regionalibus a decessore Nostro sanctae memoriae latas Nobisque approbatas, in omnes partes diligenter servari volumus et jubemus, ita ut in seminariorum regimine, disciplina, ac studiis nihil immutatum censeatur." Benedict XV, Motu Proprio "Seminario clericorum," Nov. 4, 1915, A. A. S., VII (1915), 495.

and expects in discipline, study, and administration. They include a Programme of Studies proposed by the Congregation of Bishops and Regulars, on May 10, 1907,[64] and a compilation of disciplinary norms proposed by the same Congregation on January 18, 1908.[65] A further argument may be drawn from the permission given by Pope Benedict XV, in 1921, to the Sulpicians, by which they were given the privilege in perpetuum of assuming charge of seminaries without previously obtaining the consent of the Holy See.[66] The necessity of such permission is nowhere mentioned in the Code and if the Pontiff granted an exception from it in 1921, the assumption is that the pre-Code law concerning the transfer of seminaries to religious institutes or congregations still retains its legal force.

There is a sharp divergence of opinion among canonists after the Code, however, concerning this important restriction of episcopal authority. Cappello [67] infers that where there is no derogation from the general law, the Bishop may transfer his seminary to an Institute or Congregation without the intervention of the Holy See. This opinion is openly advocated by Vermeersch-Creusen,[68] and by Woywod.[69] There is no doubt that the transfer of seminary jurisdiction was a serious derogation from the law of the Council of Trent, which did not advert to the possibility of such a contingency.[70] It manifestly intended the seminary to be in the hands of the diocesan clergy, and a transfer would be an infringement of their rights.[71] Moreover, there were usually clauses not only restricting the rights of the present Bishop, but also preventing his successors from withdrawing the seminary from the Institute.[72] Cappello and Vermeersch evidently think that there is not necessarily the same derogation from the Code legislation, and that the purpose of the law consequently vanishes except in particular cases. The implication is that where the end of the law is absent, the law does not bind. This objection can be answered from an analysis of the decisions and interpretations on this matter.

---

[64] A. S. S., XL, (1907) 336

[65] A. S. S., XLI (1908) 212.

[66] A. A. S., XIV (1922), 37-40.

[67] *Summa Juris Canonici* II, 380.

[68] *Epitome*, II, 408.

[69] *Commentary*, II, 116.

[70] A. S. S., III (1911), 61.

[71] Lucidi, *De Visitatione*, II, 346.

[72] Lucidi, *loc. cit.*; Bouix, *De Episcopo*, II, 73.

In the first place, the opinion of these canonists is in contravention to the principle, "*Finis legis non cadit sub lege.*" The mere fact that the intention of the legislator in promulgating a law is not verified in a particular instance does not thereby exempt from the law.[73] The genesis of the law has been treated in the historical synopsis. The principal element in its formation was custom, which was implicitly approved by the constant modus agendi of the Holy See. A definite expression of the law was finally given by the Congregation of Bishops and Regulars. In approving the constitutions of the Mission Congregation of St. Francis de Sales, it stated that Bishops could not give the direction of seminaries to regular orders or other institutes without the permission of the Holy See.[74] In 1861 the Congregation amplified this statement to comprise a fuller description of the law by plainly stating the obligation to secure permission of the Holy See in every case, even where the institute has been approved for the very purpose of seminary administration.[75] There is absolutely nothing in the words of the Congregation to warrant the interpretation that where there is no derogation is it not necessary to bring the case to the Holy See. Otherwise the provision that permission be asked ". . . *in singulis casibus* . . ." would be meaningless.

Prior to the Code, canonists claimed no such exemption. Lucidi,[76] Bouix,[77] Pouan,[78] Vecchiotti,[79] Ferraris,[80] and Wernz,[81] all treat the question at some length, and merely declare unequivocally that the Holy See must be consulted whenever such a transfer is contemplated. This was evidently the accepted interpretation, and it has been adopted by some eminent modern canonists; e. g., Cocchi,[82] Ojetti,[83] and Bargilliat.[84] The opinion prevalent before the Code was that the diocesan clergy should be entrusted with the supervision of the seminary, in order that its best interests might be served, and that the requisite episcopal supervision might be secured and safeguarded.

---

[73] Noldin, *De Principiis Theologiae Moralis*, p. 196.
[74] Bizzarri, *Collectanea EE. et RR.*, p. 797.
[75] Bizzarri, *op. cit.*, p. 790.
[76] *De Visitatione*, II, 347.
[77] *De Episcopo*, II, 73.
[78] *De Seminario Clericorum*, p. 219.
[79] *Institutiones Canonicae*, II, 180.
[80] *Bibliotheca*, v. seminarium, nn. 198-99.
[81] *Jus Decretalium*, III, 92.
[82] *Commentarium*, VI, 93.
[83] *Synopsis*, n. 3674.
[84] *Praelectiones Juris Canonici*, n. 267.

The very nature of a religious institute would necessitate certain concessions,[85] and the power of the Bishop would become inevitably weakened in some way, at least indirectly.[86] The preponderance of the evidence, together with the opposition of so many canonists, would seem to render untenable the position of Vermeersch, Cappello, and Woywod. The only case in which the intervention of the Holy See is unnecessary is when the privilege of assuming charge of seminaries without it has been granted by Pontifical indult. The Sulpicians enjoy this privilege in perpetuum, and may administer seminaries without the usual commissions, although dependent upon the Bishop, to whom they must render an annual report.[87]

Bouix outlines the proper mode of procedure for the transfer of a seminary to a religious institute.[88] The Ordinary and the religious Superior should first determine upon certain articles of agreement which are to govern their future relations and the administration of the seminary. This should then be submitted to the Holy See for confirmation and approbation. The perpetuity of these agreements will vary in individual cases, although Bouix contends that the successors of the Bishop are usually bound to retain the religious supervision. Vermeersch [89] indicates the following as usual conditions: that the Superior General appoint the Rector and the deputies; that there be no commissions; that the supervision be perpetual, so that there can be no arbitrary recession from the agrement. De Meester [90] cites as an example a permission granted by Pope Clement XI, in 1708. The first article concedes the administration perpetually, and reserves other rights to the Bishop; the second provides that the Fathers be supported from the seminary revenues; the third prescribes a monthly meeting of the Bishop and the seminary officials; the fourth clause refers to financial matters; and the fifth provides for the annual report to the Bishop. The latter, together with the right of the Bishop to visit the seminary, have always been indispensable to obtain the permission of the Holy See. An unedited decree of the

---

[85] Bouix, *De Episcopo*, II, 73; Idem, *De Capitulis*, p. 444; A. S. S., III, 54 (footnote).

[86] Thomassinus, *Nova et Vetus Disciplina Ecclesiastica*, II, I, c. 102, n. 6; Pignatelli, Consultationes Canonicae, IX, cons. 81, n. 152; Micheletti, *De Regimine*, p. 53.

[87] A. A. S., XIV (1922), 37.

[88] *loc. cit.*

[89] Vermeersch-Creusen, *Epitome*, II, 408.

[90] *Compendium Juris Canonici*, II, 287.

Congregation of the Council refused this permission to the Bishop of Culm in 1680 because the Lazarists would not take charge of the seminary unless exempt from a report of their administration.[91] Vermeersch aptly suggests that the stipulations for the transfer be so clear and precise that there will be no cause for arguments or for regret.[92] The decisions of the Congregation of the Council on this matter also required the Bishop to secure the consent, not only of the deputies, but also of the Chapter, before applying for permission.[93] The necessity of securing the permission of the Holy See for the withdrawal of a seminary from the supervision of religious will depend solely on the terms of the agreement. The question arises whether any permission is required for a Bishop to appoint a religious or a member of a Congregation to a position as Rector or other official without, however, transferring the administration of the seminary to the order or congregation. The code does not legislate directly for this particular case. However, the appointment of a religious as an official of a diocesan seminary would involve a permanent departure from the environment of his religious institute, and the provisions of canon 638 concerning exclaustration and secularization can be applied. The canon refers both to religious orders and to congregations.[94] Therefore, when the society is of pontifical right, an indult would have to be secured from the Holy See before one of its members could assume a position as official of a diocesan seminary. The Ordinary is competent to grant such permission when the society is of diocesan right. Several unedited decrees of the Congregation of Bishops and Regulars, issued before the Code, record refusals of permission on the grounds that such a procedure is contrary to the spirit of a religious institute, and that it is very liable to cause dissatisfaction among the diocesan clergy.[95] Pope Pius X, however, in a letter to the Superior of the Lazarists, empowered him to permit his subjects without restriction to assume the duties of officials in the seminaries of Italy.[96]

Most of the decrees of the Holy See between the Council of

---

[91] A. J. P., IX, 603.

[92] *Epitome*, II, 408.

[93] S. C. C. in Spoletana, Sept. 22, 1714—A. J. P., IX, 619; Wernz, *Jus Decretalium*, III, 92.

[94] Piontek, *De Indulto Exclaustrationis necnon Saecularizationis*, p. 76.

[95] S. C. EE. et RR., April 28, 1806—A. J. P., XVI, 741; Idem, Dec. 18, 1769—A. J. P. XIV, 1011.

[96] May 22, 1904, A. S. S., XXXIX, 136.

Trent and the Code which contain restrictions of episcopal power present problems of finance, with which this dissertation is not concerned directly. A few decrees on administration pertain to the deputies, but these have already been mentioned in the historical legal development, since the general law concerning these officials has been changed in the Code. With reference to erection, the Congregation of Bishops and Regulars decreed that the Seminary could not be placed in the dwellings of the canons without their permission, and even then the students were to have no communications with the canons.[97] The erection of the so-called "*mixed*" seminaries has been expressly reprobated many times. The Congregation of the Consistory condemned them, in 1912, as detrimental to sacerdotal vocations,[98] and the Instruction issued to the Ordinaries of Italy, in 1920, further demands that Ordinaries provide other schools, separate and distinct in discipline and studies, for those who intend to embrace the ecclesiastical state.[99] The same condemnation has been voiced by many Pontiffs,[100] and has been confirmed by Pope Pius XI, in a letter to Cardinal Bisleti, Prefect of the Congregation of Seminaries,[101] The transfer of the seminary from the cathedral city to another site is subject to the approval of the Holy See.[102] Such a procedure should be contemplated only for very grave reasons.

The Congregation of Bishops and Regulars was asked, in 1727, whether the Bishop had to render to anyone an account of the expenditures of the seminary.[103] The reply was that such a report must be made to the metropolitan, ". . prout *de jure*," although no particular time was mentioned for its rendition. The legal basis of the decision was the section of the Tridentine decree which imposed upon metropolitans the duty to secure the observance of the decree among their suffragans. Such an obligation could not be urged since the Code. However, canon 734 §4 gives to metro-

[97] In Mutinen., (1604)—Ferraris, *Bibliotheca*, v. seminarium, n. 5.

[98] "La promiscuitá di alunni non chiamati e di altri alunni chiamati allo stato ecclesiastico riesce sempre fatale a questi alunni e . . . causa la perditá di molte vocazione."—Il Monitore Ecclesiastico, III, 144.

[99] *Ordinamento dei Seminari*, April 26, 1920, pp. 7-8.

[100] Pope Leo XIII, Encyc. "*Paternae*," Sept. 14, 1899—Fontes, n. 643; Pope Pius X, "*Pieni l'animo*," July 20, 1906,—Fontes, n. 676.

[101] August, 1922, A. A. S. XIV, 449.

[102] S. C. C. in Melivitana., July 9, 1725—Pallotini, v. *seminarium*, § n. 26; in Terracinen., Aug. 24, 1816—*Thes.* S. C. C., LXXVI, 215.

[103] In Naulen., A. J. P. XI, 622.

politans the right to exercise a vigilant care for the preservation of correct ecclesiastical discipline in their suffragan dioceses. This implies a knowledge of the status of the various diocesan seminaries, but the metropolitan could not urge any legal obligation on the part of the suffragan Bishops to make any periodic report, nor interfere with their administration of diocesan seminaries. St. Charles advised the rendition of such a report twice a year.[104]

Canon 1357.—§2. Potissimum studeat episcopus frequenter Seminarium ipse per se visitare, in institutionem quae alumnis traditur sive litterariam et scientificam, sive ecclesiasticam sedulo vigilare, et de alumnorum indole, pietate, vocatione, ac profectu pleniorem sibi comparare notitiam, maxime occasione sacrarum ordinationum.

The Code here prescribes personal visitations of the seminary by the Bishop, without, however, making any definite determination concerning their frequency. The Tridentine decree also used the term *frequenter,* and this or its synonym, *saepe,* usually appears in subsequent legislation. Both words have been subject to varied interpretations. There is certainly no limitation to the number of visits a Bishop may make. According to a decision of the Congregation of the Council, the Bishop may visit the seminary as often as he desires, and this same right is accorded to the Vicar Capitular and administrator when the See is vacant.[105] Pope Benedict XIV interprets *frequenter* as meaning a monthly visit.[106] The Council of Naples, in 1699, considered it to mean every two months.[107] St. Charles, with his usual conservative attitude, gives the more liberal interpretation of every three months.[108] The saintly Bishop thus made a general visitation twice a year, accompanied by the two commissions, on the feast of the Nativity of the Blessed Virgin and at Easter. The remaining visit, evidently informal, was made at his convenience. This programme satisfies sufficiently the rule of frequent visitation, without any undue monopoly of the time of the Bishop. It must be noted that the Code specifically states that these visits are to be made by the Bishop himself. It is a personal onus and can be discharged by no one but the Bishop. Cappello

[104] *Acta Ecclesiae Mediolanensis,* I, 211.
[105] S. C. C. in Vigelevanen. Jan. 13, 1704—A. J. P., IX, 616; Lucidi, *De Visitatione,* II, c. VI, n. 38.
[106] *Institutiones Ecclesiasticae,* cons. LIX, n. 16, II, 233.
[107] Coll. Lac., I, 299 d.
[108] *Acta Ecclesiae Mediolanensis,* I, 58.

holds that it is a grave obligation.[109] These visitations are distinct from the quinquennial visitation of canon 343 §1, in which, however, seminaries are to be included.[110]

The purpose of the visitation is evident from the context. The personal contact thus established not only enables the Bishop to discover directly the material needs of the seminary, but is also intended as a method whereby he may discharge his obligation to maintain a watchful care over the training of the students. This vigilance must extend to the minor seminary also, as the Code indicates from the phrase ". . . *institutionem . . . litterariam et scientificam* . . ." The principal objective of the visitation, therefore, will usually be to assure the Bishop of the observance of the norms directive of study and discipline which paragraph three of this canon orders to be formulated. It may also be the means of securing a more intimate knowledge of the students. The Bishop, as the chief shepherd of his diocese, has a grave obligation to safeguard the spiritual welfare of the faithful. He is thus bound to protect the integrity of the Priesthood by ordaining only those candidates who are deemed fit and worthy of this exalted office. This presupposes a previous knowledge of their character, piety, vocation and learning. However, it does not seem practical for the Bishop to interview individual students on the occasion of his visitations. A fair and correct estimate of piety or learning could hardly be gained in this manner. It would be much better to rely on the knowledge secured from a prudent Rector or Spiritual Director, who comes into daily contact with the student.[111] When their opinion is unfavorable, the Bishop might personally interview the student before taking action. The intellectual ability of the students could best be ascertained from a survey of the marks given them by their professors, rather than through a personal examination by the Bishop.

These considerations indicate the procedure to be followed on such visitations. The Bishop should inspect the entire building, paying special attention to necessary improvements or repairs. There should be a meeting of the disciplinary commission and of the professors to discuss matters of discipline and study and a meeting of

---

[109] *Summa Juris Canonici*, II, 387.
[110] Lucidi, *De Visitatione*, II, c. VI, n. 123.
[111] Pius X, Motu Proprio, "*Sacrorum Antistitum*," Sept. 8, 1907—A. A. S., II (1910), 666.

the commission on temporal administration, attended also by the econome, to discuss financial matters. The Rector should be present at both these meetings. There should also be an interview with the Spiritual Director. The Bishop might well give a general conference to the students, in which he could make any necessary or advisable observations concerning study and discipline. Moreover, when the time for ordination approaches, the Bishop should give a conference to the candidates, calling to their attention the dignity of the office they are about to assume; the regulations they will be required to observe on the mission; diocesan statutes pertaining to the clergy, and other relevant subjects. It would also be well to have the diocesan statutes and faculties explained to the ordinands by one of the professors.

Canon 1357.—§3. Unumquodque Seminarium suas leges habeat ab Episcopo approbatas, in quibus quid agere, quid observare debeant, doceantur tum qui in eodem Seminario in spem Ecclesiae instituuntur, tum qui in horum institutionem operam suam impendunt.

Bishop Hedley has well said: "No community can exist, much less can it exist prosperously, without a common rule."[112] Order is a fundamental necessity in any society, and the very purpose and character of seminary life render it all the more necessary that the duties of the students, together with their relations with each other and with their superiors, be governed by some definite regulations. These rules will affect indirectly the Superiors and professors. The Code, however, by the phrase ". . *qui . . . . . operam suam impendunt,*" requires that there be also some formal delineation of the rights and duties of the seminary officials.[113] The use of the term *unumquodque* indicates that this paragraph is applicable both to major and to minor seminaries,[114] although there will necessarily be some variation. The burden of constructing the rules does not necessarily fall upon the Bishop. The Code merely says that they should be approved by the Bishop, and therefore they may be formulated by the members of the commissions or by the Rector. This method was suggested by the Third Plenary Council of Baltimore.[115]

---

[112] *Lex Levitarum,* p. 66.
[113] Cocchi, *Commentarium,* VI, 92.
[114] Cappello, *Summa Juris Canonici,* II, 400; Conc. Bituricensis (1850) tit. III—Coll. Lac., IV, 1109 c.
[115] *Acta Concilii Plenarii Baltimorensis* III, n. 151.

Some definite disposition should be made of every hour of the day.[116] Spiritual exercises, study, class, and recreation, each should have its proper place in the daily life of the student, and a prudent norm of life will obviate any undue or disproportionate emphasis upon any one of these phases of seminary life. The Bishop, in approving the curriculum, and in making such regulations as he himself deems necessary for the welfare and progress of the seminary, should be guided not only by the provisions of the Code, but also by the suggestions of the Popes and the decrees of the Congregations,[117] and by the practice of those noted for efficient seminary direction. Due consideration must be taken, however, of conditions peculiar to the individual diocese.[118]

Two things are principally necessary in a Priest—probity of life and learning.[119] As has been mentioned previously, the acquisition of these forms the first two objectives of seminary administration. In both cases, certain things must be done by the students, and as a corollary, by the officials and professors—the *quid agere* of 1357, §3. The first portion of the rule, therefore, will comprise an enumeration and description of the actions to be performed by the student during the course of the day; for example, the spiritual exercises, study and classes, and in general the daily schedule of duties.[120] The second will deal with the officials and professors. These regulations will be discussed in the commentary on canon 1358. The third part will present other regulations destined to aid the student in getting the full benefit from the training given him. This is the *quid observare* of canon 1357, §3. Micheletti makes several other apt suggestions concerning the rule. It may be composed either in Latin in the vernacular, although the latter would seem to be preferable. Portions of the rule should be read at stated intervals. However, those things which pertain directly to the officials should not be made known to the students.

Certain exercises have been prescribed as essential to foster piety and virtue in the students. Therefore the provisions of canon 1367 must be incorporated in the rule. The first paragraph of this canon

[116] Council of Bordeaux (1850) tit. V—Coll. Lac., IV, 591 c.

[117] Micheletti, *De Regimine Seminariorum*, p. 146.

[118] Pius IX, *Letter to Bishops of Austria*, Nov. 5, 1855—Coll. Lac., V, 1240 a.

[119] *Acta Ecclesiae Mediolanensis*, II, 875; Pius X, Motu Proprio, "*Sacrorum Antistitum*," Sept. 8, 1907—A. A. S., II, 666.

[120] Micheletti, *De Regimine Seminariorum*, p. 146.

deals with the daily spiritual exercises to be performed in common: e.g. Morning and evening prayers, meditation, and assistance at Holy Mass. The length of time allotted for these various exercises will depend on the disposition of the remainder of the day, and on the time assigned for rising and retiring. Even when speaking of clerics in general the Code does not determine the time to be spent in meditation,[121] from twenty minutes to a half hour would seem to be a reasonable and not too lengthy period to spend in an exercise that is deemed of such importance by spiritual writers. Other exercises, however, should also have their place in the horarium: e.g. visit to the Blessed Sacrament, the recitation of the Rosary, examination of conscience, both particular and general, and spiritual reading.[122] The recitation of the Angelus is also a salutary custom. A certain time should be set apart during the week for the hearing of the students' confessions, although they should be free to go at any time, if they so desire. Some day other than Saturday should be chosen for this, in order to facilitate the coming of priests from outside to hear confessions, according to the provisions of canon 1361. The students should receive Communion frequently, and should be so urged in conferences. However, no attempt should be made to transgress the limits of individual liberty of conscience.[123] Solemn Mass and Vespers should be celebrated for the community on Sundays and Holydays. On these same days, if at all possible, some students should be assigned to the Cathedral church for ceremonies. This practice promotes a knowledge of the Sacred Liturgy, especially concerning pontifical functions; it accustoms the student to appearing in public ceremonies; it engenders in him a desire to perform the rubrics accurately, and in the people a just pride in their students for the Priesthood. Provision should also be made for an annual retreat, the duration of which is left to the discretion of the Bishop. Three days should be a minimum, five a maximum.[124] The schedule for the retreat should be so constructed that the students will have sufficient time for meditation on the subject of the retreat conferences and on their own spiritual state.

Due time must also be assigned to study and to classes. The

---

[121] Canon 125 § 2.
[122] Canon 125 § 2.
[123] Cocchi, *Commentarium*, VI, 106.
[124] Instr. Cong. EE. et RR. to Ordinaries of Italy (1908)—*Anal. Ecc.*, (1908) p. 107.

Priest is to be the leader and the teacher of the people—the light of the world; and especially in our own day there is need of a learned Priesthood.[125] It is not within the province of this dissertation to discuss the programme of studies in detail. The provisions of canons 1364, 1365 and 1366 will, of course, form its basis. On May 10, 1907, the Congregation of Bishops and Regulars decreed that the scholastic year in Italy should not be less than nine months.[126] Certainly it should not be longer than that period, which should comprise also time spent in examination. As far as the number of students in each class is concerned, Micheletti[127] very properly contends that a class should be kept below forty members to ensure efficient teaching. If it is necessary to have over forty in a class some division should be made. The horarium of classes and study should be drafted by the Rector or Prefect of Studies, with the counsel and advice of the professors[128] and of the commission on discipline. The Congregation of Bishops and Regulars,[129] and the Congregation of the Consistory, in a letter to the Ordinaries of Italy,[130] both declare that there should not be more than four hours of class a day. They also suggest that one day a week, other than Sunday, should be free. A larger schedule of classes does not seem feasible in view of the time that must be spent in the other exercises of the day. Care must be taken to safeguard the health of the students by permitting sufficient recreation. There should also be sufficient time for study. The matter taught in class will be assimilated much more readily if the student has an opportunity to review it in his room; to see its correlation with other parts of the Catholic system of philosophy or theology; and in general, to exercise his intellect rather than merely his memory. Too much stress cannot be laid on the need for adequate study time. All these considerations involve as their corrollary the obligation of the students to perform the spiritual exercises mentioned, to attend classes faithfully and at-

125 "Lumen doctrinae, neque illud vulgare, in sacerdote requiritur, quia munus ejus est implere sapientia ceteros, evellere errores, ducem esse multitudini per itinera vitae ancipitia et lubrica."—Leo XIII, Encyc. "*Exeunte jam anno*," Dec. 1, 1888, Fontes, 602.

126 Bargilliat, *Monita et Decreta*, p. 175.

127 *De Ratione Studiorum*, p. 37.

128 Micheletti, *op. cit.*, p. 39.

129 *Programme of Studies for the Seminaries of Italy*, May 10, 1907—A. S. S., XL (1907) 336.

130 July 16, 1912, A. A. S. (1912), 491; Le Canoniste Contemporain, XXXV, 593.

tentively, and to visualize well the time given them, whether for study or for recreation.

In addition to the active programme outlined above, the Bishop should also delineate certain things to be observed with regard not only to the performance of the actions described, but also to conduct, demeanor, dress, relations of the seminarians with their superiors and among themselves, and other things of a like nature. The Code contains nothing definite concerning these things, which are left to the prudence of the Bishop. A few suggestions for this portion of the rule can be taken from the Institutes of St. Charles and from the decrees of the Congregation of Bishops and Regulars.[131] The proper reverence and obedience must always be shown to the Rector and the other officials. The places assigned to each student in the chapel, refectory, and class-room, should not be changed arbitrarily by them. All the common exercises should be attended punctually. Silence should be observed at certain stated times. This is especially true of retreat time, when one should commune with God and with self, but not with his fellows. Moreover, studies are also repugnant to the spirit of a retreat, which should therefore be given at the beginning of the year or after the mid-year examinations. All absences from spiritual exercises and classes should be reported to the proper authorities.

The discipline of the seminary should not be too rigorous, nor yet engender a laxity of life and thought which later might prove detrimental to the ministry of the Priest. Above all, the authorities should instill into the students a proper attitude toward the rule. Its purpose and necessity should be explained—its sole purpose is to render them better fitted for the state to which they aspire, and to mold them more closely to Him they seek to serve. Prudence should be exercised in its administration. The Third Plenary Council of Baltimore wisely advises the superiors of seminaries to be discreet in their vigilance for the observance of the rule.[132] An intemperate zeal for the observance of the rule, especially in its minor and secondary provisions, may have a harmful effect on the spirit of the students, who will consider it not as the yoke of Christ but rather as a burdensome bond.

---

[131] *Acta Ecclesiae Mediolanensis*, II, 875-78; Bargilliat, *Monita et Decreta*, pp. 202-06.

[132] *Acta Concilii Plenarii Baltimorensis* III, n. 158.

Canon 1357—§4. Seminarii interdiocesani vel regionalis regimen universum et administratio regitur normis a Sancta Sede statutis.

The Council of Trent, foreseeing that certain circumstances might prevent the constitution of a diocesan seminary, prescribed that the dioceses of a province could combine to institute a common house of studies for clerical students, in the event that each could not have its own seminary. These are called provincial or regional seminaries. Canon 1359, §4 specifically reserves the constitution and the formation of administrative regulations for these seminaries to the Holy See. The intervention of the Holy See is necessitated by the possibility of a conflict of rights or duties between the metropolitan and the suffragans concerning the selection of officials and deputies, financial matters, visitations, and other things of a like nature.[133] The very fact that the Code states no fixed rules in this matter implies the probability of variation with each individual case, and precludes any absolute statement of norms for their government. Certain legal provisions from various sources, however, provide us with a general indication of the modus agendi of the Holy See in this matter.

The Congegation of the Council, July 9, 1921, in a decree dealing with the case of a canon teaching in a regional seminary, affirmed that there is a recognized fiction of law whereby a regional seminary is considered legally just as a diocesan seminary.[134] This principle was approved by Pope Pius XI, in a letter to Cardinal Bisleti, in which the Pontiff also stated as a corollary that each Bishop might consider the regional seminary as his own.[135] The presumption is, therefore, that the duties of the officials and the provisions of the general law regarding the spiritual exercises and ratio studiorum will remain the same as for diocesan seminaries. The individual Bishops would retain the right to visit at will their own students. The seminary would also enjoy the privilege of parochial exemption.[136] Concerning

[133] A. J. P. I, 1074.
[134] A. A. S., XVI (1924), 399.
[135] "At vero par est et consentaneum, sacrorum quoque Antistites, qui ejus sint regionis, cujus gratia Seminarium hujusmodi sit incitatum, debere omnes eidem pro virili parte prospicere. Etenim si reputaverint—quod res est—suam cujusque causam hic agi, et seminarium interdiocesanum vel regionale suarumque cuique diocesium seminarii majoris instar esse, in quo ipsi eadem jura eademque officia singuli habeant . . . ," August 1, 1922, A. A. S. XIV, (1922), 449.
[136] Cappello, *Summa Juris Canonici*, II, 401.

other matters we must refer to several documents issued by the Holy See, which either actually constitute a regional seminary or give norms for their direction.

The regional seminaries of Italy are governed by a college of Bishops composed of those who rule dioceses in the province, and these constitute a substitute for the usual commissions. They meet every month to examine the report of the Rector, and the Bishop in whose diocese the seminary is instituted is entrusted with the task of seeing that the provisions deemed necessary by the council are rendered effective.[137] The Third Plenary Council of Baltimore passed practically indentical provisions for the United States.[138] The most complete available document on the constitution of a regional seminary is an Apostolic Constitution of Pope Pius X, which approved the erection of such an institution in Calabria.[139] The decree premitted each Ordinary of the province to consider the seminary as his own, with regard to the students from his diocese, with the privilege of visiting it whenever they desired. To preserve discipline, however, no individual Ordinary could issue orders or regulations, even for his own clerics, without the consent of the Rector. The Archbishop and the Bishops were to meet once a year for a consultation on the needs and problems of the seminary. It was further provided that three of the Bishops should constitute a special commission, to which the Rector should come for advice concerning administrative problems. The seminary was expressly exempt from parochial jurisdiction. The nomination of the Rector was reserved to the Holy See, together with that of Spiritual Director and the Prefect of Studies. The selection of the other officials was left to the council of Bishops. The Bishops could either ordain their own clerics or grant the necessary dimissorials. In everything else the seminary was to be governed by the general law.

The Congregation of Seminaries instituted an interdiocesan seminary on June 15, 1928, because of the union of two dioceses under one Bishop.[140] The only noteworthy departure from the general law was that the election of the Deputies had to be preceded by a consultation with the chapters of both dioceses.

---

[137] Bargilliat, *Monita et Decreta*, pp. 180-81.
[138] *Acta et Decreta*, n. 167, n. 156.
[139] May 5, 1914—A. A. S., VI (1914), 213 ss.
[140] A. A. S. XXI, (1929), 571.

Cocchi holds that the constitution of a regional seminary may be accomplished either through a formal decree of the Congregation of Seminaries, or by the approval granted by the Congregation of the Council to the acts of a provincial Council which provide for the erection of such a seminary.[141] However, canon 256, §1 grants exclusive competence to the Congregation of Seminaries in matters relative to the administration of seminaries, including the approval of their erection. The wide extent of the competence vested in the Congregation is evident from a decision which concedes to it the faculty of conceding permission to alienate seminary goods.[142] The approval of the acts of a provincial council by the Congregation of the Council, therefore, would not seem to be sufficient for the erection of a regional seminary. Augustine[143] contends that when a regional or provincial seminary has been instituted, the Bishops of the province must send their clerical students there, and are no longer permitted to send their students to another seminary. Vermeersch denies this interpretation of canon 1354, §3.[144] Cocchi[145] rightly holds that while there may be no strict obligation to send the students to a provincial seminary, it is certainly the mind of the Church in constituting them that the Bishops of the province send their students to study there. Both Cocchi and Vermeersch admit that the particular norms stated in the decree of erection may settle the question in individual instances.

The fiction of law previously mentioned, whereby a regional seminary may be considered as a diocesan seminary, may have far reaching effects. It was a determining factor in the solution of a case concerning incardination presented to the Congregation of the Council.[146] A certain student, having received the proper dimissorial letters from the Bishop in whose diocese he desired to serve, entered the regional seminary erected by that diocese and several others for their respective students, and received tonsure from the Bishop in whose city the regional seminary was situated. He subsequently received the remaining orders, and was ordained to the Priesthood for the diocese in which he had been incardinated,

---

[141] *Commentarium*, VI, 87.
[142] Dec. 7, 1922—A. A. S., XV (1922), 40, ad. 4.
[143] *Commentary on the Code of Canon Law*, VI, 379.
[144] *Epitome*, II, 387.
[145] *Commentarium*, VI, 87.
[146] Mar. 10, 1923, A. A. S., XVI (1924), 51.

although he had never dwelt there and had never even been there. He then claimed that he belonged to the diocese of his origin. The Congregation decided that he belonged to the diocese in which he had been incardinated, and among the decisive arguments adduced was that he actually had acquired a legal domicile in the diocese for which he was incardinated, even though he had never been there. The very fact that he had dwelt in the regional seminary was accorded the same legal value as if he had been dwelling in a diocesan seminary in the diocese of incardination.

CHAPTER SIX

Seminary Officials

The complex character of seminary discipline, and the diversity of objects it seeks to attain, render it necessary to divide its immediate direction among various officials. The Trident decree makes mention of no officials save professors. The constitution of the others mentioned in this canon represents a necessary development in seminary organization; a development which, like so many others, can be traced to St. Charles Borromeo.[1] It is apparent from post-Tridentine legislation that his example was followed almost universally.[2] The econome is not mentioned so frequently in Congregational decisions and in Pontifical documents as the Rector, the professors and the Spiritual Director. The latter office was sometimes designated merely by the word *confessarius*.[3] Virtually all the Councils held in the past two centuries have passed decrees concerning the constitution of these officials, and the frequency of their appearance in decisions of the Holy See seems to be an explicit approval of them. The Code presents for the first time, however, general legislation demanding their appointment.

The selection of the officials is a prerogative of the Bishop,[4] although this is one of the cases in which the advice of the deputies should be asked. Capello [5] says that this canon is not preceptive, although he asserts that one of its provisions, namely that the econome should be distinct from the rector, does contain a precept. It would

---

[1] *Acta Ecclesiae Mediolanensis*, II, 867-74.

[2] S. C. C. in Fundana, Mar. 26, 1689—Pallotini, v. *seminarium*, § 2, n. 17; in Lucana, Jan. 20, 1838, n. 20; Leo XIII, Encycl., "*Quod multum*," Aug. 22, 1886—Fontes, n. 594; S. C. C. in Aquinaten—Thes. S. C. C., CIII, pp. 72, 197, 201; Conventus EE. Bavariae, 1850—Coll. Lac. V, 1176 b; Conc. Remensis, 1849—Coll. Lac., IV, 133 c.

[3] *Acta Ecclesiae Mediolanensis*, II, 870; Council of Venice, 1859, c. XVI —Coll. Lac., VII, 313 b.

[4] Council of Trent, Sess., XXIII, *re ref*. c. 18, Buckley, *Canons and Decrees of the Council of Trent*, p. 175; S. C. C. in Mediolanen—Ferraris, *Bibliotheca*, v. seminarium, n. 52; Wernz, *Jus Decretalium*, III, 92; Pius X, Litt. Encyc. "*Pieni l'animo*," July 28, 1906—Fontes, n. 676; Pius X, Litt. Encyc. "*Pascendi*," Sept. 8, 1907—Fontes, n. 680; Pius IX, Ep. encyc. "*Singulari quidem*," Mar. 17, 1856—Fontes, n. 521.

[5] *Summa Juris Canonici*, II, 388.

seem more logical to consider the entire canon as preceptive. Certainly the formula for the triennial report made to the Congregation of Seminaries takes for granted that these officials have been appointed.[6] Therefore, while the opinion of Capello might constitute sufficient grounds for not observing the canon, the Holy See is evidently desirous that it be followed in both major and minor seminaries.[7]

Although the functions of the various officials demand certain peculiar and appropriate characteristics in each individual, there are certain qualities that are requisite for all. These are mentioned in canon 1360, §1. The first is that they be of sound doctrine. It is patent how great danger would encompass the faith of our Catholic people, and how futile it would be to hope for the proper propagation of the faith, if priests were not sufficiently conversant with sound Catholic doctrine, or adhered to and expounded erroneous opinions or theories concering it. The logical preventive of this is to safeguard the doctrinal integrity of clerical education from its very inception. Hence the Popes have deemed it expedient again and again to reiterate the exhortation that Bishops exercise extreme care in the selection of seminary officials, whose example and teaching are of such primary importance in the formation of future priests.[8] The insidious character of modern errors, especially in the fields of philosophy and theology, demands that the student build his intellectual structure on a firm foundation of orthodoxy. This is impossible unless the seminary superiors possess the requisite learning —a learning which must have orthodoxy as one of its principal constituent elements.

Knowledge and orthodoxy, however, are not sufficient. The Code further demands that seminary superiors be endowed with the virtues essential to their office, especially with that of prudence.

---

[6] A. A. S., XVII (1925), 549.

[7] Cocchi, *Commentarium*, VI, 92; Cappello, *Summa Juris Canonici*, II, 365.

[8] "In iis maxime evigelent curae et cogitationes vestrae; efficite ut litteris disciplinisque tradendis lecti viri praeficientur, in quibus doctrinae sanitas cum morum innocentia conjuncta sit, ut in re tanti momenti iis confidere jure optimo possitis. Rectores disciplinae, magistros pietatis eligite prudentia, consilio, rerum usu prae ceteros commendatos . . ."—Leo XIII, Ep. encycl. "*Quod multum*," Aug. 22, 1886—Fontes, n. 594; Idem, Ep. encycl. "*Providentissimus Deus*," Nov. 18, 1893—Fontes, n. 621; Pius X, litt. encycl. "*Pascendigregis*," Sept. 8, 1907—Fontes, n. 680; Idem, Motu proprio "*Sacrorum Antistitum*," Sept. 1, 1910—Fontes, n. 689; Pius IX, Ep. encycl. "*Nostis et nobiscum*," Dec. 8, 1849—Fontes, n. 508.

The education of the seminarian is not only intellectual—it is also spiritual, and all education is vitalized by example. In seeking to acquire virtue, the student naturally observes those upon whom the sacerdotal character has already been impressed, and seeks to imitate them in the practical exercise of the principles of the spiritual and ascetic life. Superiors, therefore, whether their province be discipline or study, must possess a deep spirit of faith, which will necessarily be reflected in a profound reverence in speech when dealing with sacred things, and of action, especially in chapel, when celebrating Mass, on ceremonies, and in all actions connected with the liturgical worship of the Church. They should strive always to be just in their evaluation of students, considering impartially their good qualities and defects, their actions, and circumstances that might mitigate or aggravate their faults and breaches of rule. The influence of natural prejudices and passion should be minimized as much as possible. The seminary superiors should also be animated by an earnest zeal for the proper performance of the duties entrusted to them, prompted by the realization that they are the sculptors chosen to mold the facile minds and hearts of untrained youths into worthy reproductions of their Divine Master. However, zeal must be tempered with prudence, and the importance of the latter is such that it is the only virtue specifically mentioned in this canon. Great and irreparable harm might be done by an imprudent or hasty judgment of a student, or by an unduly precipitate mode of action. Yet they must be careful not to carry virtues like prudence and mildness to such an extreme that the student may feel that he can disregard with impunity any phase of seminary discipline. Nor are the foregoing considerations to be dismissed as mere idealism, for they are a logical development of the phrase used by the Code itself, ". . . . *etiam virtutibus ac prudentia praestantes* . . .". Canon 1360, §1 also prescribes that the seminary officials be selected from among priests. This is necessitated by the very character of such offices as those of the Rector, Spiritual Director and Confessors. However, lay professors and economes might be permitted under certain circumstances. St. Charles makes the practical suggestion that the officials be chosen from among those who have pursued their studies in the diocesan seminary.[9]

---

[9] *Acta Ecclesiae Mediolanensis,* II, 867; Cocchi, *Commentarium,* VI, 93.

Some difficulties are presented in the selection of a canon as a seminary official. This question can best be considered under two general aspects: first, the choice of the Canon Theologian, Canon Penitentiary, or some other canon as a professor in the seminary; secondly, their choice as one of the other officials mentioned in canon 1358. By virtue of his office, the Canon Theologian has the duty of proposing a public explanation of the Sacred Scriptures at a definite time on stated days.[10] The Bishop, for a grave cause, may substitute for this the duty of teaching in the seminary.[11] Wernz-Vidal holds that the Theologian can satisfy by either method the demands of his office,[12] and this opinion has been upheld by a decision of the Congregation of the Council, July 19, 1921.[13] The decision held that if the Theologian taught in the seminary by mandate of the Bishop he thereby fulfilled the duties of his office, and was entitled to the fruits of his prebend and also to the daily distributions, by virtue of canon 420, §1, n. 2. The decree further stated that he was also excused from the appplication of the conventual Mass. These privileges can be enjoyed, however, only on those days when the Theologian is actually engaged in teaching, unless a special indult has been secured.

The office of the Canon Penitentiary, unlike that of the Theologian, bears no relation to teaching.[14] Nevertheless, he may be deputed to teach Theology or Canon Law in the Seminary,[15] in which case he is exempt from choir, but receives only the revenues from his prebend, and has no portion in the daily distributions. Moreover, this privilege may be enjoyed only on days when actually teaching.[16] In a Spanish case submitted to the Congregation of the Council in 1923, the argument was advanced that teaching in a seminary could be considered a part of the duty of the Canon Penitentiary in Spain, by virtue of the Gregorian Constitution. In the latter document Pope Gregory XV sanctioned the fiction of law whereby a Penitentiary obliged to treat a case of conscience for an hour every day was considered as present in choir. The Congre-

10 Canon 400 § 1.
11 Canon 400 § 3.
12 *De Personis*, p. 746.
13 A. A. S., XIV (1924), 397.
14 Canon 401 § 1.
15 Canon 421 § 1, n. 1.
16 Commission for the Interpretation of the Code, Nov. 24, 1918—Il Monitore Ecclesiastico, XXXI, 175.

gation decided the case solely according to Code legislation, and denied the right of the Penitentiary to particpate in the daily distributions.[17] Wernz-Vidal believes that the legislation regarding the loss of distributions by canons engaged in other duties is based on the supposition that they will receive an appropriate remuneration for such duties.[18] Canon 421 §1, n. 1 excuses from choir those who teach Theology or Canon Law. The Pontifical Commission has interpreted this canon as including such branches of sacred science as Church History, Liturgy, and Sacred Scripture.[19] It might also be extended to include Philosophy, the handmaid and foundation of Theology. Ordinary members of the Chapter might be deputed to act as professors in the seminary under conditions similar to those just mentioned concerning the Penitentiary. The office of a canon would seem wholly incompatible with that of any other of the seminary officials. The administration of the seminary demands the entire time and attention of the latter, and any practical coordination of the duties of a canon and those of a Rector or Econome would be extremely difficult. The law of residence could not be observed, nor attendance at community exercises, and canons 420 and 421 do not mention the function of a seminary official among the causes excusing from these regulations.

The Bishop has the right to remove the seminary officials whenever he so desires, although such a removal should always be prompted by a just and equitable cause, and should be preceded by a consultation with the deputies.[20] Ojetti[21] and Micheletti[22] mention the following causes which might persuade the removal of an official: chronic illness; old age; discord among the officials themselves, or between an official and the students; bad example by a superior; the necessity of transferring a superior to another position; and lastly, the promotion of an official. According to canon 2403, an official refusing to make the usual profession of faith may, after a monition, be removed from office. A seminary official may have

---

[17] A. A. S., XVII (1925), 510.

[18] *De Personis*, p. 748.

[19] Nov. 24, 1920, A. A. S., XII (1920), 593.

[20] Wernz, *Jus Decretalium*, III, 92; Pouan, *De Seminario Clericorum*, p. 211; Cappello, *Summa Juris Canonici*, II, 388; S. C. C. in Tricarien., Mar. 24, 1735—Pallotini, v. *seminarium*, § 2, n. 2; Idem, in Lucana, Jan., 1838, Pallotini, *loc. cit.*, n. 3.

[21] *Synopsis*, n. 3673.

[22] *De Regimine*, pp. 253-54.

recourse from the decree of a Bishop only to the Congregation of Seminaries.[23]

1. *The Rector.*—The seminary represents a union of diverse individuals, each with differing duties and personal characteristics, into one society, and hence the primary principle of order demands the constitution of a recognized superior. Supreme authority over the seminary is exercised by the Bishop, but the Code wisely prescribes the selection of a Rector as his immediate representative in the supervision of the internal government and discipline of the seminary. Besides the qualities previously mentioned as requisite for all officials, the Rector should be more advanced in age, in order better to command respect and obedience; skilled in all matters pertinent to clerical discipline, and able to supervise intelligently both the discipline and temporal affairs of the seminary.[24]. The office naturally demands a high degree of executive ability, and its dignity and importance presuppose an incumbent of the highest character. Not only the students but also all officials of whatever status are subordinate to the Rector, and the Code enjoins upon them the precept of obedience in whatever pertains to the functions proper to their respective offices.[25] The Rector, however, is entirely dependent upon the Bishop, and can make no drastic change in discipline or policy without first securing episcopal approbation. The selection of a properly qualified incumbent for the office should enable the Bishop to grant to him a certain amount of autonomy in the administration of discipline, in securing the observance of the regulations, and in supervising the work of the other officials. Canon 1360, §2 seems to imply this, for the Rector cannot be expected to consult the Bishop in every action and decision. He should be empowered to use his prudent judgment in matters pertinent to general discipline, making a report of any action taken if he deems it necessary. Some authors extend this even to permit the Rector to expel a student who has committed a serious public transgression,[26] provided he immediately informs the Bishop of his action. Even though this action might seem warranted, some effort should always be made to secure the approbation of the Bishop.

[23] Canon 1601.
[24] *Acta Ecclesiae Mediolanensis*, II, 867.
[25] Canons 1360 § 2 and 1369 § 1.
[26] Augustine, *Commentary*, VI, 392; Micheletti, *Constitutiones Clericalium*, p. 15.

The office of a seminary Rector would seem to be an ecclesiastical office in the strict canonical acceptance of the term. It is duly constituted by law in canon 1358, and thereby acquires a certain objective stability. Moreover, there is attached to it a measure of jurisdiction. Cappello [27] divides the element of jurisdiction into jurisdiction properly so called, and an administrative power to which no real jurisdiction is attached, and considers either sufficient for a canonical office. The office of seminary Rector can be assimilated to both these classes. Canon 1368 expressly attributes to the seminary Rector the rights of a pastor over those who are in the seminary, with some restriction in the matter of marriages, and in the hearing of students' confessions, and the office of a pastor is considered a canonical office.[28] Moreover, if a church is attached to the seminary the Rector of the seminary is considered as the Rector of the church, unless the Ordinary should provide otherwise.[29] The administrative power exercised by the seminary Rector is undeniable, for this is the very reason for the constitution of the office. These considerations seem sufficient to constitute a probable opinion that he holds a canonical office, in which case his appointment will be subject to the canons in the Code which deal with ecclesiastical offices.[30]

The present Apostolic Delegate to the United States, in a letter to Ordinaries of this country,[31] has given a brief but expressive delineation of the function of a seminary Rector:

> The general government of the seminary, and in a special manner the training of the students in the discipline of the Church, are the particular tasks of the Rector, in dependence always on the Ordinary. The Rector should so order all things that the different parts of the seminary will work together in harmony to its true and final purpose—the formation of priests according to the spirit of Jesus Christ. The spirit of charity should govern the seminary . . . . . making it one family of which the Rector is the father . .

Other sources present a more detailed analysis of the duties of the Rector. Canon 1369 states that his first obligation is to secure

[27] *Summa Juris Canonici*, I, 269.
[28] Cappello, *op. cit.*, *loc. cit.*; Vermeersch-Creusen, *Epitome*, I, 181; Maroto, *Institutiones Juris Canonici*, p. 676; Wernz-Vidal, *Jus de Personis*, p. 169.
[29] Canon 480, §3.
[30] Canons 145 to 195.
[31] AER, LXXIX, 82-83.

the observance of the seminary regulations. This also applies to the other officials, although the duties of the econome, confessors, and Spiritual Director preclude direct and constant activity in this matter. Therefore, the rules should be read to the students at least once every semester by either the Rector or the Vice-Rector, and they should also address the students briefly from time to time concerning prevalent breaches of rule, exhorting them to a more faithful observance of it.[32] St. Alphonsus[33] advises that the Rector observe personally the actions of the students, e.g. in the refectory, at recreation, and in the classroom. St. Charles[34] suggests that he have frequent consultations with the other officials concerning the students and matters of discipline.

The Rector is also obliged to see that the requirements of the curriculum of studies are observed. Even where the immediate supervision of its organization and practical operation has been entrusted to a Prefect of Studies, the authority of the Rector is in nowise diminished, and he should still maintain a close contact with the problems and progress of the curriculum.[35] He should examine frequently the class standings of the students, visit the classes from time to time, and assist at examinations if he deems it expedient. A report of the scholastic standing of the students should be submitted to the Bishop at least every semester. Where it is not feasible to have both a Rector and Prefect of Studies, the former usually assumes the immediate direction of the curriculum. This involves the formation of the programme to be followed in the various classes, after a consultation with the professors. Their advice should also be sought concerning an appropriate disposition of days and hours of class. No excessive burden of classes should be placed upon any individual professor, for this is not only unfair to the professor, but also proves detrimental to the students. The Rector should also supervise the grading of the students and their organization in the various classes. The professors should submit the matter for examinations to him. The former should be consulted concerning the establishment of a fair and standard passing mark for promotion to higher classes.

[32] S. C. EE. et RR., *Normae pro seminariis Italiae*—A. S. S., XLI, 212.
[33] *Reglement pour les Seminaires*, p. 436.
[34] *Acta Ecclesiae Mediolanensis*, II, 869.
[35] Micheletti, *De Ratione Studiorum*, p. 163; S. C. EE. et RR., *Normae pro Seminariis Italiae*, (1908)—A. S. S., XLI, 218.

Canon 1369, §2 renders it further incumbent upon the Rector or his assistants to instruct the students in the laws of refinement, courtesy and politeness. The priest is the accredited represenative of the Church, and many of those outside the Church will evaluate it according to the character of the priests with whom they come into contact. The priest should therefore be known to the world as a gentleman of refinement and culture, familiar at least with the ordinary and sensible canons that govern good manners. The discourteous priest, or one who fails to observe the common rules of politeness, may be a positive injury to the Church.[36] The consequences possible from the actions of such a priest are too harmful to ignore, and some effort must be made to obviate them by proper seminary training. Therefore the Code prescribes the teaching of *Christian* urbanity. The refinement of the priest must be rooted in the realization that, before everything else, he is another Christ. The imitation of Christ is the ultimate norm of conduct for a priest, and it is a norm which demands for its observance a far higher perfection than the world requires for its code of conduct. The primary source of Christian urbanity will be the social aspects of the life of Christ, as they appear in the Sacred Scriptures and in the works of the commentators. This fundamental knowledge may be further developed by a consideration and coordination of certain principles of Catholic philosophy and theology governing our conduct toward our fellow men. This will furnish a proper background for a practical consideration of urbanity, not only in its relation to the ordinary social conventions, but also in its particular relation to the priestly state. The students should be instructed in proper methods of expression, both in speech and in writing; they should be taught proper formulae for introductions and other occasions; correct table manners; conventional clerical dress; and proper modes of action to be followed under certain circumstances, as in the matter of interviews with the laity in rectory offices. These matters cannot be considered as trivial or non-essential, for they are indispensable to the priest in his social contacts both with the faithful and with those outside the Church. Some formal instruction in clerical urbanity should therefore be given, either by the Rector himself, or by one of the professors. The Spiritual Director might also make it the subject matter of some of his discourses to the students.

[36] Smith, *The Training of a Priest*, p. 86.

Canon 1369, §2 also prescribes an exhortation to the students upon the truth and intrinsic merit of the trite aphorism concerning Godliness and cleanliness. The Congregation of Bishops and Regulars placed this burden especially upon the Rector and Vice-Rector.[37] Detailed regulations have also been given concerning precautions to safeguard the health of the students, and the duties of the physician and infirmarian. Places frequented by the students should be large, well aired, and sufficiently lighted. There should be sufficient closet room to enable the students to keep their clothes neat and clean. Moreover, the solicitude of the Code should be reflected in every seminary by the installation of modern and adequate equipment for bathing, and also for laundering. The students should be advised to recreate, as far as possible, in the open air. When prevented from so doing by inclement weather, there should be proper provisions made for indoor exercise. The seminary doctor should come on stated days, and the students should have free access to him for treatment and advice. He should have the privilege of making suggestions to the Rector concerning necessary hygienic precautions or preventives. An infirmary should also be established where students my receive medical care and treatment.

Besides the right, previously mentioned, to the obedience of the other officials, the Rector also has the duty to see that each is faithfully discharging the duties of his office. However, there should be no such detailed surveillance as would hamper them in their work. It is sufficient if he receives from them a periodic report,[38] subsequently giving them the benefit of his advice, direction, and guidance. The moderators mentioned in canon 1369, §3 for the supervision of the work of the professors should be restricted to the Rector or Vice-Rector. The methods already mentioned of supervising the curriculum will preclude any continuing heterodoxy in teaching. The regular attendance of professors at their classes may be presupposed. When a professor is forced to omit a class, he should acquaint the competent official of the intended omission. The students can then be notified, and confusion will be averted. The Rector should take cognizance of whatever suggestions are made

---

[37] *Normae pro seminariis Italiae,* art. 33—A. S. S., XLI, p. 219.

[38] A. S. S., XLI, p. 218.

by the other officials for the good of the seminary, putting them into effect wherever possible and advisable.[39]

According to canon 358, §1, the Rector as least of the major seminary has the right to participate in the diocesan synod, and the initial words of the canon indicate that he also has an obligation to attend. Canon 1406, §1, n. 1 renders it obligatory for him to make the usual profession of faith when attending such a synod, even though he has previously made it at the beginning of the scholastic year or at the beginning of his term of office as Rector, as canon 1406, §1, n. 7 prescribes. At the end of every scholastic year he should make a report of the status of the seminary, from the viewpoint of discipline, study, hygiene, and temporal administration.[40] The Tridentine decree had demanded that the Bishop receive an annual report only of the financial status of the seminary, in the presence of the commission on temporal administration. This report was made by the Rector or by the econome.[41] It is evidently not the intention of the Code that the Rector be the immediate administrator of the goods accruing to the seminary.[42] The requirements of canon 1523 would be incompatible with his office, and moreover, canon 1358 provides for an official to perform this office. However, he should be cognizant of the financial status of the seminary funds and revenues, and should therefore be present at the meetings of the Bishop with the commission on temporal administration. The expenditures made by the econome should be approved by the Rector. The obligation to render an annual account of the expenditures made by the Rector and the econome may be inferred from canon 1525. Canon 1649 empowers the Rector to represent the seminary in court.

By virtue of the exemption of the seminary from parochial jurisdiction,[43] the Rector possesses all the rights of a pastor over those who dwell therein, with the exception of certain restrictions concerning the Sacraments of Matrimony and Penance. The seminary remains territorially within the limits of the parish in which it is

[39] A. S. S., XLI, p. 218.

[40] S. C. C. in Fundana, Mar. 26, 1889—Pallotini, v. *seminarium*, §2, n. 17; A. S. S., XLI, p. 219, art. 36.

[41] S. C. C. in Fundana, Mar. 26, 1689—Pallotini, v. *seminarium*, §2, n. 17; in Aquinaten., Nov. 27, 1852, Idem, §4, n. 2; Pouan, *De Seminario Clericorum*, p. 300.

[42] Vromant, *De Bonis Ecclesiae Temporalibus*, p. 199.

[43] Canon 1368.

situated, and only the pastor of the place or his delegate can validly assist at marriages clebrated there.[44] Neither has the Rector the unrestricted right to hear the confessions of the students. He may hear their confessions only when they spontaneously seek him out for that purpose, and when there is a grave and urgent cause.[45] Cappello[46] cites as a grave cause the desire of the penitent to acquire peace of conscience under circumstances which make it relatively necessary to approach the Rector. This condition may be considered verified by the very fact that a student approaches the Rector of his own accord. The same author holds that there is a grave obligation to observe this canon, and to abstain from the habitual hearing of confessions. The reason for the restriction of canon 891 is obvious. The integrity of the sacramental seal must be safeguarded, and it would be completely subversive of discipline and order if the Rector was harassed in his administrative duties by a constant conflict between the internal and external fora. These considerations would apply also to the Vice-Rector.[47] Vermeersch contends that the Rector of the seminary has ordinary power to hear the confessions of the students.[48] Cappello[49] asserts that this opinion lacks intrinsic probability, and adduces convincing arguments. It seems logical that if the Rector possessed ordinary jurisdiction he would be able to use it under ordinary circumstances. Therefore, while he may be considered as having ordinary jurisdiction in the matter of confession over others attached to the seminary, the Code evidently places the seminarians in the same category as the nuns attached to the seminary, over whom, as pastor, he does not exercise ordinary jurisdiction for confessions.

The Rector may exercise parochial rights over all those who are within the seminary, whether major or minor. The exemption concurs with the legitimate erection of the seminary, and canonists agree that it is also extended to villas, where it is the custom for the seminarians to spend a portion of the summer vacation in such institutions.[50] The phrase *pro omnibus qui in seminario sunt* seems

[44] Canon 1368; Cappello, *Summa Juris Canonici*, II, 402.
[45] Canon 891.
[46] *De Sacramentis*, II, 333.
[47] Cappello, *Summa Juris Canonici*, II, 389.
[48] Jus Pontificium, II (1921), 67.
[49] *De Sacramentis*, II, 304.
[50] Augustine, *Commentary*, VI, 407; Il Monitore Ecclesiastico, VIII (1924), 179; Vermeersch-Creusen, *Epitome*, II, 405; Cappello, *op. cit.*, II, 403.

to be of wider scope than the term *familiaris*, and therefore, while the latter is restricted to those who dwell continually in a community,[51] the common opinion is that the former comprises not only those who dwell in the seminary habitually, such as the students, but also servants and others who work in the seminary, but do not live there. Those who remain in the seminary for only a portion of the day, however, enjoy the privilege of exemption only for the period of time that they actually spend in it.[52] The Rector may perform for his subjects the following acts, by virtue of his office as pastor: administer the Sacraments, including Viaticum and Extreme Unction; dispense from the laws of fast and abstinence, and from the observance of feasts of obligation;[53] and perform the usual funeral services, with all the rights and duties attached thereto.[54] If the funeral ceremonies for those who actually live within the seminary are performed in some other church, the Rector of the seminary can claim the parochial portion.[55] His parochial rights do not entitle the Rector to interfere in any way with the internal organization of the religious community of women who are often assigned to a seminary to care for the material welfare of the students. The selection of such a community, and the duration of their charge, depends solely upon the Bishop.[56] The confessions of the community will be governed by the general provisions of the Code.[57]

The obligation of the Bishop to ordain only those whom he considers to have a vocation to the sacerdotal state, and who are worthy and capable of such an office, has been mentioned in the preceding chapter. To discharge this obligation effectively, he must depend to a great degree upon the seminary Rector, who should ensure the observance of the provisions of the Code concerning ordinations, particularly with reference to the absence of any irregularities or impediments. Because of the many requests for release from the

---

[51] CPR, VI (1925), 137.

[52] Cocchi, *Commentarium*, VI, 108; Vermeersch-Creusen, *Epitome*, II, 432; Cappello, *Summa Juris Canonici*, II, 402.

[53] Canon 1245, §1.

[54] Fanfani, *De Jure Parochorum*, pp. 264, 267, 315; *Vermeersch-Creusen, Epitome*, II, 405; Cappello, *Summa Juris Canonici*, II, 402; canons 1215 and 1222.

[55] Ferry, *Stole Fees*, p. 100.

[56] Micheletti, *Constitutiones Seminariorum Clericalium*, p. 40; Cocchi, *op. cit.*, VI, 109.

[57] Canons 520 ss.

obligations of sacred orders, the Congregation of the Sacraments has issued an instruction containing certain norms intended to aid the Bishop and the seminary Rector to ascertain more accurately the presence of a vocation and the absence of impediments. Two months before the reception of tonsure and minor orders, the candidate must present a written petition, signed by himself, and testifying that he seeks them voluntarily. The petition is then sent to the Bishop, together with the testimony of the Rector and of the other seminary officials concerning the qualities, aptitude, and vocation of the candidate. In particular cases the pastor of the candidate may be required to give a similar testimony, according to a formula appended to the instruction. All the documents are to be preserved in the diocesan archives. If necessary, the same process is to be followed before the candidate receives the subdiaconate. If no canonical reason hinders the reception of major orders, the candidate must write out a petition, according to the formula in the instruction, stating that he approaches sacred orders voluntarily, is cognizant of their duties and obligations, and is willing to observe them. The declaration must be accompanied by an oath, given before the Ordinary or his representative. The same process is to be followed before the reception of diaconate and priesthood. The instruction must be read to the students at the beginning of every scholastic year.[57a]

2. *The Professors.*—The Tridentine decree provided for the appointment of professors by the Bishop, or at least with his approval, and further stated that the preference should be given to those who had received a doctorate or licentiate in Theology or Canon Law, although others competent to teach were not excluded.[58] This is substantially the background of the Code legislation. Canon 1366, §1 renders it incumbent upon the Bihsop, with the advice of the disciplinary commission, to select the seminary professors. Although the canon also states that the preference should be given to one possessing at least a licentiate in Theology or Canon Law, the phrase *ceteris paribus* implies that such a degree is not essential. No degree could adequately compensate for a lack of ability or interest

[57a] Dec. 27, 1930—A. A. S., XXIII (1931), 120-29.

[58] Sess. XXIII, *de ref.*, c. 18—Buckley, *Canons and Decrees of the Council of Trent*, p. 175.

in teaching. Cappello rightly insists that the code does not here intend to include honorary degrees in Theology or Canon Law.[59] Moreover, the degree must be obtained from a University or Faculty duly constituted by the Holy See,[60] and endowed with the requisite permission to confer academic degrees that are canonically effective.[61] The only faculty member for whom a degree is absolutely necessary is the professor of Sacred Scripture. Pope Pius XI, in a Motu proprio of April 27, 1924, decreed that no one should teach Sacred Scripture in a seminary unless he had received at least a baccalaureate degree from the Biblical Institute.[62] This stress upon the importance of degrees implies an obligation for individual Bishops to send a certain number of students to pursue a course of studies in an approved university.[63]

Frances[64] and Micheletti[65] have compiled classic delineations of the requisites for a professor. The former first postulates in him the virtue of charity. He must always be mindful of the fact that his pupils do not know as much about the subject he is teaching as he does, and he should be tolerant of their mistakes; he must be just, prudent, faithful to the high commission entrusted to him, and must possess to a great degree the virtue of equanimity. Frances also suggests that youthful professors be chosen to serve with older men on the seminary faculty. Micheletti summarizes the qualities of a professor under four heads: *knowledge* of the subjects to be taught, which can be gained only by assiduous study, and by a familiarity with the literature proper to them, especially that which is recent or current; *orthodoxy; zeal* and *application*, both in the preparation of class lectures and in attendance at class; *ability to preserve discipline* and order in the classroom.

The Congregation of Bishops and Regulars, May 10, 1907,[66] declared that each subject in the departments of Theology and Philosophy should be taught by a different professor, or that a professor should be given at least cognate subjects to teach. The use of the term *saltem* in canon 1366 §3 shows that this is still the mind

59 *Summa Juris Canonici*, II, 390.
60 Canons 256, §1 and 1376.
61 Canon 1377.
62 A. A. S., XVI (1924), p. 180.
63 Micheletti, *De Ratione Studiorum*, p. 181.
64 *De Ecclesiis Cathedralibus*, p. 505.
65 *Op. cit.*, pp. 203-05.
66 Bargilliat, *Monita et Decreta*, p. 175.

of the Church. However, the canon obliges the selection of separate professors only for Sacred Scripture, Dogmatic Theology, Moral Theology, and Ecclesiastical history. Cappello contends that this is not a strict obligation.[67] This is true in the sense that when a paucity of professors or some other valid reason renders it difficult or practically impossible to fulfill the provisions of the canon, there is certainly no obligation. The distribution of the curriculum of studies will necessarily vary according to the number of available professors and the number of hours each is required to teach. Professors of Theology, Canon Law, and Philosophy must make the prescribed profession of faith at the beginning of every year, or at least when they first assume their place on the seminary faculty.[68] The Congregation of the Holy Office, on March 22, 1918,[69] decreed that the provisions of the Motu proprio "*Sacrorum Antistitum*" of Pope Pius X,[70] concerning the oath against Modernism, retained their force even after the promulgation of the Code. Therefore, the seminary professors should repeat the oath, according to the prescribed formula, at the beginning of every scholastic year.[71] The professors must make known to the Bishop the text-book which they are to use in class.[72] This may be done through the medium of the annual report of the Rector. Canon 1366 §2 prescribes that theological and philosophical studies be pursued according to the principles and methods of St. Thomas Aquinas. This does not necessarily exclude systematic text-books which contain a composite presentation of orthodox theological thought,[73] nor does it sanction and approve in their entirety the opinions of the Angelic Doctor.[74] Lectures in the departments of theology and philosophy should be delivered in Latin,[75] but it would seem eminently practical to supplement these with an exposition in the vernacular of the matter treated.

The Code contains no prohibition against the appointment of lay

---

67 *Summa Juris Canonici*, II, 391.
68 Canon 1406, §1, n. 7.
69 A. A. S., X (1918), 136.
70 Sept. 1, 1910—Fontes, n. 639.
71 S. C. Consist., Sept. 25, 1910—A. A. S., II (1910), 740.
72 Pius X, Motu proprio "*Sacrorum Antistitum*," Sept. 1, 1910—Fontes, n. 689; Cappello, *Summa Juris Canonici*, II, 390.
73 Augustine, *Commentary*, VI, 402.
74 Pius XI, Litt. encyc. "*Studiorum ducem*," June 29, 1923—A. A. S., XV (1923), 309; LQ (1922), p. 648.
75 " . . . latine et tradendae et percipiendae sunt." Letter of Pope Pius XI to Cardinal Bisleti, Aug. 1, 1922—A. A. S., XIV (1922), 453.

professors to the seminary, but the advisability of such a procedure is questionable. It certainly seems much more appropriate that clerics receive their entire training from those already in the clerical state.[76] The Congregation of the Council, in 1838, decided that the removal of a lay professor, presumably merely because he was a layman, was not illegal.[77] This indicates that it is more consonant with the mind of the Holy See to have clerical professors. However, under certain circumstances it may be necessary to have a lay professor on the seminary faculty. The Bishop and the Rector should then investigate thoroughly the character, knowledge and teaching ability of the candidate, and once appointed, the Rector should see that he is treated with every courtesy and consideration. Members of religious orders may also be permitted to teach in diocesan seminaries. If it is necessary for such a professor to remain outside the religious community, an indult of exclaustration must be secured.[78] When a professed religious returns to the world, however, even though he possesses an indult of secularization, he cannot teach in either a major or a minor seminary without a special indult from the Holy See.[79] This is true even for those who have had only temporary vows, or who have merely made an oath of perseverance, provided they have lived under the obligation of these promises for a period of six full years.[80]

The delicate matter of salaries has scarcely been touched in ecclesiastical legislation on seminaries. Certainly some adequate recompense should be made to seminary professors for their voluntary sacrifice of the daily ministry to the faithful, the very essence of priestly life, in order to assume the arduous task of teaching. The Apostolic Delegate to the United States, in a recent pronouncement, adverts to this question,[81] and requests the Ordinaries to secure for their seminary professors such a salary as will relieve them of all economic necessity, leaving them free to take the means necessary to develop and perfect themselves in chosen fields of study. The Delegate suggests a suitable and progressively increasing scale in salaries.

[76] Micheletti, *De Ratione Studiorum*, p. 184; Lucidi, *De Visitatione*, II, 364, n. 59.
[77] In Lucana, (1838)—Pallotini, v. *seminarium*, §2, nn. 3-4.
[78] Canon 638.
[79] Canon 642, §1, n. 2.
[80] Canon 642, §2.
[81] AER, LXXIX, 82-83.

The Code makes no provision for the duration in office of the seminary professors, and their tenure will depend on the will of the Bishop. The decisions of the Congregation of the Council present absolute unanimity in conceding to the Bishop discretionary power in the removal of professors.[82] From these decisions it appears, however, that the Bishop is expected to have a just and reasonable cause,[83] such as have already been mentioned for officials in general. Canonical equity demands this, especially when a professor has been on the seminary faculty for some years. A cause for removal not previously mentioned, which applies to the other officials but particularly to the professors, to whom is entrusted the actual formal education of the students, is heterodoxy, or even the suspicion of it, especially with reference to Modernism. The Congregation of the Holy Office specifically mentioned it as a cause for removal to the Ordinaries of Italy, in 1907,[84] and Pope Pius X extended the provisions of the Congregation to the entire Church.[85] Micheletti [86] makes the practical suggestion that the removal of a professor should be made at a time when his successor may make fitting preparations to assume the office. The Bishop, therefore, unless absolutely necessary, should not remove a professor until the close of the scholastic year.

3. *The Econome.*—Canon 1358 briefly describes the econome as instituted to care for the material needs of the seminary. The Congregation of Bishops has declared that his office is chiefly to supervise the material direction and financial management of the house, although he remains dependent upon the Rector.[87] From these two brief descriptions it appears that the function of the seminary econome is usually limited to a direct and immediate supervision of necessary financial expenditures. This would include such things as the purchase of food, the payment of servants' salaries, the making of necessary repairs, and other incidental disbursements. This, at least, seems to be the significance of the phrase *pro curanda re familiari.* Moreover, the internal management of temporalities is the only phase of financial

---

[82] In Agrineten., Dec. 11, 1875—AJP, XV, 354; in Spoletana, June 22, 1844—Pallotini, v. *seminarium,* §2, n. 6; in Tricarien., Mar. 22, 1735—Idem, n. 2.

[83] Lucidi, *De Visitatione,* II, 366.

[84] A. S. S., XL, 727.

[85] Encycl. "*Pascendi,*" Sept. 8, 1907—Fontes, n. 680.

[86] *De Regimine,* p. 261.

[87] "All' Economo spetta, sotto la dipendenza del Rettore, l'interna gestione finanzaria e materiale del Seminario.", art. 71, A. S. S., XLI, 223.

administration which would logically come within the competence of the Rector to direct. The duties of the econome, however, may vary according to the extent of administrative power granted to him by the Bishop.[88] Besides the merely internal administration, the econome may also be given complete supervision over the finances of the seminary—the acquisition of funds, their investment, the acceptance and payment of notes, and similar matters.[89]

Whatever the competence of the econome, he would seem to be bound by the provisions of the Code concerning administrators. Although as a procurator, whose province only comprises the care of the daily economic needs of the institution, he cannot be considered as an administrator in the full legal sense, yet his power of buying and selling, however restricted, is an administrative function.[90] It is an important part of the powers ordinarily attributed to ecclesiastical administrators, and the purpose of the legislation in canons 1527, 1528, and 1529 is thereby verified, namely to regulate the conservation and proper disposition of ecclesiastical goods. According to canon 18, therefore, the procurator would be subject to their provisions. This renders it necessary for the seminary econome to take an oath before the Ordinary or Vicar Foreane to fulfill his commission worthily,[91] namely with fidelity and with prudence.[92] He should keep an up-to-date and accurate account of the funds entrusted to him by an approved method of bookkeeping,[93] and these records should be kept in a safe place.[94] Besides the periodic account of expenditures rendered to the Rector,[95] an annual account must be rendered to the Bishop, either by the Rector in his general report, or by the econome himself, if he is the legal administrator of the seminary funds.[96] An inventory should be taken when the econome assumes office, according to canon 1522 §2. If such an inventory has already been recently taken by a predecessor, it should be sufficient

88 Micheletti, *De Regimine*, pp. 518, 523.
89 Canon 1523; Micheletti, *op. cit.*, pp. 519-22.
90 Vromant, *De Bonis Ecclesiae Temporalibus*, p. 185.
91 Canon 1522, §1.
92 Micheletti, *De Regimine*, p. 207.
93 Canon 1523, §5.
94 Canon 1523, §6.
95 Council of Bordeaux (1850), tit. V.—Coll. Lac., IV, 592d; Council of Rheims (1849), tit. XIV.—Coll. Lac., IV, 133 b; S. C. EE. et RR. (1907)—A. S. S., XLI, 223.
96 Canon 1525.

for the new econome to accept it, with whatever slight changes are necessary after verification.

The econome cannot act validly outside the limits of ordinary administration [97] without the written consent of the Ordinary.[98] Moreover, the Church is not responsible for contracts entered into without the consent of the legitimate superior who, in the case of seminaries, is the Bishop. One of the principal duties of the econome will be to supervise the purchase of food. He should also visit often the various parts of the institution, in order that it may be kept in good repair.[99] The domestics and workmen should be hired by him, subject to the approval of the Rector. These people should be selected carefully as to character and capability. They should be assigned a just and living wage, and their duties should be consonant with their ability, age and sex.[100] Canon 1358 demands that the econome be distinct from the Rector, and he is excluded by canon 1359 §2 from serving on either of the advisory commissions. Canon 1521 §2 indicates that the Bishop may choose a layman as seminary econome if he so desires.

4. *The Confessors.*—Canon 1358 provides that in each seminary, whether major or minor, there be at least two ordinary confessors. In saying *at least* two, the canon indicates that there may be more than two, and the number of confessors should always be proportionate to the number of students. The office of the Spiritual Director is manifestly intended by canon 1358 to be distinct from that of a confessor, and he is not considered as one of the ordinary confessors. Yet the spiritual direction of the seminary comprises within its scope not only the spiritual welfare of the community as a whole, but also that of individual students. The latter end may often be attained very effectively through the sacramental forum. It is extremely desirable that the Spiritual Director be known to the students not only as one ready to advise them in matters relevant to vocation and conduct, but also as a confessor, who will be for their spiritual ills an understanding judge and physician.[101] It is not necessary for the confessors prescribed by canon 1358 to live in the seminary,

---

[97] Vromant, *De Bonis Ecclesiae Temporalibus*, p. 185.
[98] Canon 1527.
[99] S. C. EE. et RR., *Normae pro seminariis Italiae* (1908)—A. S. S., XLI, 224.
[100] Canon 1524.
[101] Cappello, *De Sacramentis*, II, 365.

although they should be accessible to the students at definite stated times.[102]

Since there is no prohibition in the Code, seminary professors may act as ordinary confessors. Cappello [103] rightly asserts, however, that it is not expedient for them to exercise this function. His opinion is based on sound practical reasons. A student might assume that the attitude of a professor toward him in the classroom, especially where some severity had been shown, was prompted by something he had revealed in confession. While such an unfounded suspicion would be unwarranted, there is the danger that it might arise. Moreover, the professors should be free to give their honest and candid opinion concerning the character and ability of a student. If they acted as confessors it would be difficult for them to take part in any discussion concerning such matters, and they could not vote on questions involving the admission or dismissal of clerical students.[104] When a professor habitually hears the confessions of certain students, even though he is not one of the ordinary confessors, he would still seem to be bound by the restriction of canon 1361 §3, for the purpose of the law would certainly be verified. He would thus be bound to declare the situation and to abstain from voting. Professors should therefore act only as extraordinary confessors in seminaries conducted by the secular clergy.[105] Where a seminary is in charge of religious the office of confessor may be discharged by the professors, provided they have the approval of their proper superior.

Canon 1361 §1 provides for the appointment of supplementary or extraordinary confessors. If such confessors dwell in the seminary, the students should be free to go to them whenever the discipline of the seminary permits. If they reside outside the seminary, the student can request the Rector to send for whichever one he desires to see. The Rector should make no inquiries concerning the reason for the request, nor should be exhibit any impatience or displeasure, but should immediately acquaint the confessor with the request.[106] The function of the extraordinary confessor in seminaries is analogous to that of extraordinary confessors for religious communities, and accord-

---

[102] Cappello, *Summa Juris Canonici*, II, 392.
[103] *Op. cit.*, II, 392.
[104] Canon 1361, §3.
[105] Letter of the Apostolic Delegate to the Ordinaries of the U. S., AER, LXXIX, 78; Cappello, *Summa Juris Canonici*, II, 393.
[106] Canon 1361, §2, §3.

ing to the provisions of canon 20, the former may be considered subject to the regulations of canon 521, which states that the extraordinary confessors must visit the community to which they are assigned at least four times a year.

5. *The Spiritual Director.*—The very terms by which he is designated suffice to define the office of the Spiritual Director. To him is entrusted especially the spiritual formation of the students, in order that they may attain to a greater perfection of sacerdotal life.[107] The triennial report on seminaries implies that the Spiritual Director should reside in the seminary in order properly to discharge his duties.[108] Cappello also contends that he should have no other office, unless it is absolutely subordinated to, or connected with, his work as Spiritual Director. This opinion of the eminent canonist is consonant with the provisions of the Code and of the triennial report, both of which evidently intend the Spiritual Director to exercise a peculiar office, separate from that of the other officials. Vermeersch holds that the section of the triennial report dealing with this official does not apply outside of Italy. This opinion is inexplicable, in view of the fact that the report merely seeks to enforce the provisions of the Code, which certainly binds outside of Italy. Both documents specifically say *Director Spiritus*—and the use of the singular number evidently indicates that the office should be exercised by an individual. The legislators knew of the custom existing in some countries, such as France, according to which each student may choose his own spiritual director, yet they manifestly desire that a single person be constituted in each seminary for that purpose. The opinion advanced by Vermeersch[109] is not supported by any other canonist. Blat[110] and others consider the Spiritual Director of canon 1358 as meaning but a single official. This opinion is sanctioned by the custom in many places prior to the Code.[111]

The opinion of Vermeersch is rendered further improbable by the following extract from a letter of the Apostolic Delegate to the United States to the Ordinaries of that country:

---

[107] Cocchi *Commentarium*, VI, 95; Cappello, *Summa Juris Canonici*, II, 393.

[108] A. A. S., XVII (1925), 549; Cocchi, *loc. cit.*; Cappello, *op. cit.*, *loc. cit.*

[109] *Epitome*, II, 400.

[110] *Commentarium*, III, 292.

[111] *Acta Concilii Baltimorensis* III, n. 161; *Acta Ecclesiae Mediolanensis*, II, 860.

The Spiritual Director, since he must devote all his time to the things of God and of the soul, should never, for any reason whatever, interfere with the external discipline of the seminary, neither should he occupy himself with tasks incompatible with his true work. His duty is to know the life and character of the seminarians so as to be able to give them prudent and safe advice regarding their vocations. Those who should not continue to the Priesthood, because they have not been called, he will dissuade from their intention, but those who are true to their calling he will encourage—fortiter et suaviter—to even greater efforts toward perfection. Both in private conversation and in conferences, he should speak of the dignity, the offices, and the duties of the Priesthood of Christ. He should also treat such subjects as the examination of conscience, and everything else which will assist them to develop more fully their spiritual lives.

It is likewise his duty not only to preach the need of prayer, but especially of mental prayer, and to teach students the methods of practicing such prayer. He should select for them a suitable meditation book, which all will use when they make their meditation in chapel in common. At this exercise, too, he should assist personally. It is understood also that, from time to time, instead of the reading of the meditation, he shall himself give an appropriate meditation to the seminarians. Thus he will establish them in the habit of daily meditation and will fix his work in their souls, especially for the time when his seminarians are thrown out into the many occupations and distractions which surround the work of the ministry in the United States.

From what has been written it is easy to conclude that only a person of maturity and adequate experience should be chosen for this most valuable and delicate position—a man of experience in the spiritual life—a homo Dei, one who possesses all the priestly virtues and in whom are united to charity and prudence a comprehensive knowledge of ascetic and dogmatic theology. And when such a capable person has been found . . . he should not be removed from his position except it be for the most serious reasons.[112]

---

[112] AER, LXXIX, 78.

The entire letter of the Delegate was sent with the approval of their Eminences, the Cardinals of the Congregation of Seminaries, and the above extract certainly indicates that the spiritual direction of the students is to be in the hands of a single official. Moreover, it furnishes an admirable and comprehensive summary of the requirements for the office, and little further comment is necessary. Cocchi [113] mentions that the Spiritual Director should be of outstanding discretion, gravity and devotion, well versed in spiritual discipline and in the Sacred Scriptures. He must strive to instill into the students a spirit of zeal, self-abnegation, and true obedience; extinguishing in them all desire for power or riches by salutary admonitions concerning the chief ends of their ministry, namely the glory of God and the salvation of souls.[114] He should be just as well versed in the discipline of the spiritual life as the professors are in their respective subjects. He should acquaint the Bishop with his progress and his problems on the occasion of the episcopal visitations. It should be noted that the Apostolic Delegate advises that there should be very serious reasons to warrant his removal.

[113] *Commentarium*, VI, 95.
[114] Acta Concilii Baltimorensis III, n. 161.

CHAPTER SEVEN

The Commissions

Canon 1359.—§1. Dioecesanis Seminariis bini constituantur coetus deputatorum, alter pro disciplina, alter pro administratione bonorum temporalium.

§2. Utrumque deputatorum coetum constituunt bini sacerdotes, ab Episcopo, audito Capitulo, electi; sed excluduntur Vicarius Generalis, familiares Episcopi, rector Seminarii, oeconomus, et confessarii ordinarii.

§3. Munus deputatorum per sexennium durat, nec electi sine gravi causa amoveantur; sed rursus eligi poterunt.

§4. Episcopus debet consilium deputatorum in negotiis majoris momenti petere.

1.—Constitution and Personnel

The provisions of the Tridentine decree on seminaries were so eminently practicable that the Holy See has been loath to countenance any derogations from them, except for very grave reasons. It is not surprising then, that the Code, in canon 1359, incorporates that portion of the decree which provided for the constitution of two commissions to aid the Bishop in the administration of the seminary. The centuries intervening between the Council of Trent and the new Code have shown sufficiently the wisdom and necessity of such a measure. The latter, however, makes a substantial change in the personnel of the commissions, each of which now consists of only two members. The obligation of having these commissions devolves only upon diocesan seminaries.[1] This is evident from the use of the phrase "*Dioecesanis seminariis* . . . " and is consonant with the general principle stated in canon 1357 §4. Therefore, regional or interdiocesan seminaries would be forced to constitute these commissions only if so ordered by the regulations imposed by the Holy

[1] Cappello, *Summa Juris Canonici*, II, 393; Vermeersch-Creusen, *Epitome*, II, 401.

See. Blat[2] interprets this same phrase as making it obligatory to have separate commissions for both major and minor seminaries, in dioceses where both seminaries exist. However, it would seem to be used rather in contradistinction to regional seminaries than as a comprehensive term including both major and minor seminaries. In other canons[3] the Code uses such terms as *unumquodque* and *quolibet* to signify both major and minor seminaries. The use of the plural, however, lends some verity to the opinion of Blat, which is also supported by Cocchi,[4] although, in view of the objections just mentioned, there is some doubt whether it could be urged as a strict obligation.

Paragraph two of this canon states that each commission is to consist of two priests, no mention being made of any other qualifications. The use of the definite term *sacerdotes* evidently excludes laymen and inferior clerics from serving as deputies. The choice of deputies is also otherwise restricted by the Code. Certain officials are excluded from assuming this office by virtue of the position which they already hold. The following are mentioned specifically: the Vicar General; members of the episcopal household, such as the Bishop's chaplains, secretary, or chancellor;[5] the Rector of the Seminary, its econome, and the ordinary confessors assigned to it. Canonists give substantially the same reasons for this legislation. Cappello[6] says that the Vicar General and members of the episcopal household are excluded because they really represent the person of the Bishop himself; the rest are not permitted to serve because of their intimate connection with seminary affairs, and because of the fact that in matters of dispute they would be both judges and judged. He also asserts that the appointment of these officials would be invalid. Augustine assigns the same reason for all, namely that they may preserve their independence of action. Blat[7] excludes the Vicar General and seminary officials ratione officii; the familiares of the Bishop because they would be less free in giving counsel against him. Augustine seems to give too strict an interpretation of the "familiares," since he holds that the chancellor, etc., do not come under the term when they do not actually live with the Bishop. The

[2] *Commentarium*, III, 293.
[3] cf. Canons 1357, §3, 1358.
[4] *Commentarium*, VI, 95.
[5] Augustine, *Commentary*, VI, 391.
[6] *Summa Juris Canonici*, II, 393-4.
[7] *Commentarium*, III, 295.

duties of their respective offices bring these men into constant and continuous contact with the Bishop, and the intimate dependence of their work upon his approval would render them familiares even though they should happen not to live in the same house with him.

There is no prohibition against nominating the same priest to serve on both commissions.[8] In fact, the Congregation of the Council has interpreted the Tridentine decree as permitting this cumulation of office.[9] Cappello rightly suggests that this cumulative service will often prove impractical. The same is true of the appointment of religious as members of either commission. There would be no necessity of an indult of exclaustration in this case, since the office is merely consultive and would not require a continued absence from the institute, and hence all that would be required would be the consent of the religious Superior.[10] Nevertheless, it would seem that the appointment of diocesan priests would be more in keeping with the duties of the deputies and the spirit of the Code, although if the prudent judgment of the Bishop deemed it expedient to appoint a religious, such an appointment would be legally permissible. Certainly the qualifications for the office might be found in either. The importance of their functions is sufficiently evident to prompt a careful selection of the deputies of both commissions. First of all, they should possess prudence and maturity. The members of the commission on temporal administration should also have some ability in financial matters, so that a skillful and equitable administration of seminary goods may be secured.[11]

Canon 1359 §2 states that the members of the commissions are to be selected by the Bishop, after a consultation with the members of the chapter. In the United States the diocesan consultors should be consulted. It is a moot question whether this consultation is necessary for validity or only for liceity. The interpretation of canon 105 forms the basis of the discussion. It states that where the counsel of the chapter is demanded, e.g., by the words used in canon 1359 §2, *audito capitulo*, it is *sufficient* for validity that the Superior hear the members of the chapter. Vermeersch[12] inclines to the opinion

[8] Cappello, *Summa Juris Canonici*, II, 394: Lucidi, *De Visitatione*, II, 386.

[9] Letter to the Ordinaries of Central America, March 15, 1897—A. S. S., XXIX (1897) 680.

[10] Cappello, *op. cit., loc. cit.*

[11] Vromant, *De Bonis Ecclesiae Temporalibus*, p. 201.

[12] *Epitome*, I, 151-52.

that a superior can act validly without seeking the advice of those whose counsel is demanded. He says that the Code does not determine one way or another whether the counsel is necessary for validity, since what is sufficient to act validly is not always necessary; that where counsel alone is required, which the Superior may accept or reject, the efficacy of the act depends solely from the causal element, which is the will of the Superior, and therefore, the counsel cannot be demanded as essential. He also appeals to canon 11, contending that canon 105 contains neither an express nor equivalent irritating clause; and to canon 6 §2, alleging that canon 105 completely incorporates the old law on this subject. In support of the latter contention, he cites two pre-Code canonists, Reiffenstuel and Schmalzgrueber. The former has stated that the acts of a Superior under these circumstances are nullified only when the law has attached a specifically irritating clause.[13] Schmalzgrueber is also quoted as giving a negative answer to the query whether such acts are null.[14] Wernz-Vidal[15] seems to agree with Vermeersch. He contends that canon 105 would irritate acts performed without the required counsel only if it so stated, whether expressly or equivalently, and that since it does not do so, the inference is that such acts would be only illicit. Other canonists oppose this view. Maroto,[16] Chelodi,[17] Cappello,[18] and Ayrinhac,[19] state definitely that a Superior must legitimately seek counsel when it is required by such terms as are mentioned in canon 105 §1, in order to ensure the validity of subsequent acts. Ojetti[20] also subscribes to this opinion, and has attempted a lengthy refutation of the theories of Vermeersch. Since Wernz-Vidal seems to base his opinion on the arguments of Vermeersch, the arguments of Ojetti must be given careful consideration. First of all, the context of the doubtful phrase must be considered, according to the general principle of canon 18. From the context of the phrase ". . . *satis est*," it seems obvious that is equivalent to *necessarium est*. The initial words of canon 105 are "Cum jus statuit superiorem and agendum *indigere* consensu vel consilio . . ." The term *indigere*

[13] Reiffenstuel, *Jus Canonicum Universum*, III, tit. X, n. 1, pp. 204-05.
[14] *Jus Ecclesiasticum Universum*, III, I, tit. X, n. 16.
[15] *De Personis*, p. 35, footnote 3.
[16] *Institutiones Juris Canonici*, n. 471.
[17] *Jus De Personis*, n. 102.
[18] *Summa Juris Canonici*, I, 203.
[19] *General Legislation in New Code of Canon Law*, p, 225.
[20] *Jus Pontificium*, VII (1927), pp, 13-25.

certainly implies necessity, and it is used with reference both to counsel and to consent. Moreover, the very words *satis est ad valide agendum* seem to imply necessity. The contradistinction implied in the canon is that where consent is required, the Superior cannot act validly contrary to the advice of his counsellors; where counsel only is required, he may act validly contrary to such counsel, and therefore, it is *not necessary* for validity to *follow* the advice given, but it is *sufficient* for validity to *seek* it. With reference to the objection from canon 11, Ojetti first states that if the counsel were not required for validity, the canon would be not only useless but ridiculous, inasmuch as it would destroy in its conclusion what it had stated in the beginning. Such a procedure would certainly be illogical. He later adduces a more solid canonical argument, alleging that canon 105, at least equivalently, and perhaps explicitly, irritates such acts, since in the beginning it clearly states that the case concerning which it treats is that in which the law requires either consent or counsel prior to action on the part of the Superior. The first section of this canon thus obviously deals with the requirements for validity in both cases, and just as an action contrary to expressed opinion would be invalid where consent is required, so when counsel alone is required, failure to secure it irritates subsequent action.

Ojetti further claims that both Reiffenstuel and Schmalzgrueber support his contentions. The former states that when the law requires a Superior to seek counsel, even though he be not required to follow the advice given, he must seek it under penalty of rendering his acts null.[21] Nor can such a procedure be attacked on the ground that it is useless to seek advice unless it is to be followed. The law relies upon the prudence of the Superior to determine a proper mode of action after due consideration of the opinions advanced. Such a consultation cannot but aid the Superior to form a more mature, prudent and cautious judgment. The text of Schmalzgrueber cited by Vermeersch seems to deal rather with the case where a specific mandate orders the Superior to seek advice, whereas elsewhere[22] he adheres to the common theory as proposed by Wernz:[23] "Quod consilium si in casibus a jure expressis requisitum non fuerit, acta ab

[21] *Jus Canonicum Universum*, III, tit. X, n. 10.
[22] *Jus Ecclesiasticum Universum*, III, I, tit. X, n. 9.
[23] *Jus Decretalium*, II, n. 793.

episcopo sunt irrita." The Code no longer mentions individual cases, but gives general formulae which may be applied to them. Suarez states that where a faculty of doing something with the counsel of others is granted, such counsel is a condition antecedent to the action, and pertinent to its substantial form.[24] These arguments seem much more logical and convincing than those of Vermeersch. However, since the Commission for the Interpretation of the Code has not decided the question, the opinion of Vermeersch may be followed. The adherence to it of two such eminent canonists as Vermeersch and Wernz-Vidal renders it at least extrinsically probable.

Cappello[25] alone refers to this question in connection with the election of deputies of the seminary. In accordance with his interpretation of canon 105, he postulates the consultation with the chapter as necessary for validity. When this procedure is followed, the members of the chapter or the diocesan consultors should not be questioned separately. They must be legitimately convoked and the matter placed before them in common session,[26] in which each should render his opinion honestly and sincerely.[27] This convocation is necessary for validity,[28] and the provisions of the law would not be satisfied by a separate interrogation of the individual members.

2.—*Competence of the Commissions*

The nature of the commissions must be clearly understood. They have merely an advisory right within the competence assigned to them,[29] as was the case prior to the Code.[30] The Bishop remains the final arbiter of all administrative matters. There should be no direct interference by the disciplinary commission in the internal administration and organization of the seminary, since this would be an unwarranted infringement on the competence of the Rector. The opinion of the latter should be given great consideration concerning disciplinary matters, and should be of assistance to them in the formulation of the advice they must necessarily render. In approving the selection of books, the suggestions made by the professors should

[24] *Opera omnia*, VIII, c. 13.
[25] *Summa Juris Canonici*, II, 393.
[26] Canon 105, §2.
[27] Canon 105, §3.
[28] Vernz-Vidal, *De Personis*, n. 33; Cappello, *Summa Juris Canonici*, I, 203.
[29] Cocchi, *Commentarium*, VI, 96.
[30] Wernz, *Jus Decretalium*, III, 94.

be followed as far as possible, for these men are more familiar with current literature and developments in the subjects they are teaching.

The extent of power possessed by the commission on finance presents some difficulty. It is the duty and right of the Ordinary to supervise generally the administration of the ecclesiastical goods of his diocese.[31] Authors differ as to how far this right extends, but the weight of opinion inclines to the theory that the Ordinary has the right only of exercising a vigilant supervision, which would include the right of visitation, of knowing the exact financial status of a church or institution, and even of demanding a prudent mode of administration, while the immediate administration is to be delegated to some such official as a diocesan econome.[32] Canon 1520 §1 provides for a general advisory commission to aid the Bishop in the administration of church goods, and besides this, the immediate administrators of the goods of a church or religious institution may be named either by law, by the regulations of its foundation, or by the Ordinary himself.[33] Vromant [34] holds that the immediate administrators of the goods of a seminary have been constituted by the Code itself in canon 1359 §1, and that this right has been invested in the members of the commission on temporal administration there mentioned. This does not seem to be the purpose of the Code in constituting this commission. Canon 1359 §4 specifically says that its members should be *consulted* in financial matters of grave moment. This by no means necessarily signifies that they are immediate administrators. It implies rather the opposite, namely that they are to act for the seminary in the same capacity as the general commission of canon 1520 acts for the entire diocese. Moreover, the econome is excluded from membership on this commission because he discharges a portion of the immediate administration, and therefore, would be acting as a judge in his own case. If the members of the commission were entrusted with the entire immediate administration of seminary goods, then they too would come under the same objection. The entire background of pre-Code legislation lends force to this latter view. The decree of the Council of Trent itself prescribed that the Bishop receive an annual report of the financial status of the semi-

[31] Canon 1519, §1.
[32] Vromant, *De Bonis Ecclesiae Temporalibus*, pp. 186, 194.
[33] Canon 1521, §1.
[34] *Op. cit.*, p. 199.

nary, *in the presence of* the commission on temporalities,[35] and subsequent conciliar legislation indicates that they are merely to aid in the financial administration by giving advice, not that they are actually to administer.[36]

The authority of Vromant on questions pertinent to Church temporalities is unquestionable, but the opinion contrary to that advanced by him in this matter seems to be more tenable. Some particular administrator should then be chosen in accordance with canon 1521 §1, whose function it would be to exercise ordinary acts of administration, such as the acceptance of revenues from various sources, the collection of interest on notes, buying and selling, investments, and the like.[37] The prudence of the Bishop should guide him in the selection of such an administrator, especially where it is a question of conferring this extensive power on the seminary econome. In some cases it might be found expedient to permit such financial administration to be done through the ordinary diocesan administrator, the amount accruing to the seminary being kept separate from any other revenues. Where the commission thus becomes merely an advisory body, which seems to have been the purpose of the legislator in its constitution, the members are not bound to fulfill the provisions of canon 1522, concerning the oath and inventory. This canon applies only to immediate administrators.[38] Moreover, this in nowise nullifies the power of the commission so that it is rendered useless. Even though the Code gives them only a consultive vote, their function should not be merely nominal, and their opinions should be accorded careful and weighty consideration by the Bishop.

The Code has not definitely determined the matters on which the commissions are competent to advise, and it may be presumed that they remain the same as were generally recognized before the Code. The Tridentine decree did not give a complete analysis of their respective duties, but merely indicated that one was to act as an advisory board for internal discipline; the other for financial administration. Their competence has been further determined by the

---

[35] Sess. XXIII, *de ref.*, c. 18, Buckley, *Canons and Decrees of the Council of Trent*, p. 173.

[36] Lucidi, *De Visitatione*, II, 377-87; S. C. C. in Tricarien., (1725)—Thes., S. C. C., VII, 194.

[37] Vromant, *op. cit.*, p. 185.

[38] Vermeersch-Creusen, *Epitome*, II, 482.

Congregation of the Council and by canonists.[39] The resulting synthesis of matters concerning which the commissions are to be consulted is as follows:

1.—*The Disciplinary Commission:*

1. The formation of the constitution and rules of the seminary.
2. The selection of pupils.
3. The selection of books.
4. Visitations of the seminary.
5. The dismissal of students.
6. The selection of a site for the seminary.
7. The selection of officials, and their dismissal.

2.—*The Commission on Temporalities:*

1. The determination of the amount of tax to be exacted for the seminary, etc. (Under the Code, this would include the determination of which method of raising revenue, mentioned in canon 1355, should be followed.)
2. Concerning the union of benefices.
3. The selection and dismissal of servants, etc.
4. The regulation of expenses, administration of goods and their revenues, etc.
5. The deputation of the Rector of the seminary.

The above enumeration should not be considered taxative, but merely suggestive of the matters concerning which their advice should be sought.

The same general principles which govern the interpretation of paragraph two of canon 1359 are also involved in the fourth section of the same canon, which states that the Bishop should seek the advice of the commissions in matters of great importance. Prior to the Code, several decrees of the Congregation of the Council,[40] and

---

[39] S. C. C., in Mediolanen.—Pignatelli, *Consultationes Canonicae*, cons. 81 n. 194; Ferraris, v. *seminarium*, n. 92; A. S. S., I, 693; Lucidi, *De Visitatione*, II, 387; Bouix, *De Episcopo*, II, 71; Barbosa, *Commentarium in Conc. Trid.*, p. 345; A. J. P. VII, 865; S. C. C. in Cartheginien (1597)—Pallotini, v. *seminarium*, XXX, §3, n. 3.

[40] S. C. C. in Oscensi, (1585)—Ferraris, *Bibliotheca*, v. seminarium, n. 81; S. C. C. in Fundana, Mar. 26, 1689—Pallotini, v. *seminarium*, §2, n. 17; S. C. C. in Tricarien, (1736)—*Thes.* S. C. C., VII, 194; S. C. C. in Mediolanen.—Pignatelli, *Consultationes Canonicae*, IX, cons. 81, n. 62; A. S. S., I, 693.

a consequent unanimity among canonists,[41] affirmed the necessity of this consultation with the deputies as essential for the validity of subsequent acts of the Bishop, although the latter was not considered bound to follow such advice. Pallottini avers that this is in accordance with the general legal principle that when the power of acting with the advice of others is granted, such advice is necessary for validity.[42] Some modern authors are of the opinion, however, that since the promulgation of the Code the consultation of the deputies is no longer necessary for validity. This view is taken by Cocchi,[43] Vermeersch-Creusen,[44] and Vromant.[45] The argument advanced for their position is that canon 11 precludes attaching any irritant effects to canon 1359 §4, since they contend that it contains no such invalidating clause, whether express or equivalent. This opinion fails to take cognizance of the provisions of canon 105 and canon 6, nn. 3 and 4, which are essential to a proper understanding of this section of canon 1359. The general principles previously stated concerning canon 105 would seem to be valid also in the case of canon 1359 §4. Ojetti [46] rightly construes *debet* as synonymous with *indiget* and consequently the case mentioned in canon 105 is verified here, since the law itself demands that the Superior seek counsel in certain matters. The more probable opinion would therefore render it incumbent on the Bishop to consult the deputies in order to act validly. Moreover, even the extrinsic probability attached to the opinion of certain cononists in the interpretation of canon 105 would seem to be excluded here, when canon 1359 §4 is considered in conjunction with the third and fourth sections of canon six. The initial legislation concerning the constitution of the commissions and their advisory capacity is contained, of course, in the decree of Trent. It provided merely that the Bishop should seek the advice of the commissions on matters within their respective competence, without stating in the

[41] Frances, *De Ecclesiis Cathedralibus*, p. 506, n. 274; Barbosa, *De Officio et Potestate Episcopi*, III, alleg. 77, n. 32; Van-Espen, *Jus Ecclesiasticum Universum*, II, I, tit. XI, c. 2, n. 8; *Acta Ecclesiae Mediolanensis*, I, 211; Diocesan Synod of Malines (1872), *NRT*, V. 254; Makèe, *Institutiones Juris Ecclesiastici*, I, 459; Wernz, *Jus Decretalium*, III. n. 94; Lucidi, *De Visitatione*, II, 381, n. 102; Pouan, *De Seminario Clericorum*, p. 288; Ferraris, *Bibliotheca*, v. seminarium, nn 11-12; Benedict XIV—*De Synodo*, IX, c. 7, n. 2.

[42] v. *seminarium* §4, n. 2.

[43] Commentarium, VI, 96.

[44] *Epitome*, II, 400.

[45] *De Bonis Ecclesiae Temporalibus*, p. 200.

[46] *Jus Pontificium*, VII (1927), p. 17.

substance of the law anything concerning the validity or invalidity of acts performed without such a consultation. Canon 1359 §4 contains a substantial and integral repetition of this portion of the Tridentine law, and therefore is subject to the approved and recognized pre-Code interpretation, according to the provisions of canon 6 §3. Such an authentic interpretation, promulgated by the competent authority instituted for just that purpose, the Congregation of the Council, has declared that acts of the Bishop performed without the advice of the deputies are invalid, and it has been demonstrated above that this was the constant discipline before the Code.

These considerations seem definitely conclusive and prove that even since the promulgation of the Code the Bishop acts invalidly without previous consultation with the commissions. This interpretation seems more consonant with logic and common sense, since the very purpose for which the commissions were instituted would be defeated if the Bishop could arbitrarily ignore the obligation to consult them on grave matters. This opinion has been advanced by Cappello,[47] one of the most eminent of modern canonists, who states quite definitely that the Bishop must consult the deputies before action under penalty of nullity, and also by Blat [48] and Woywod.[49] The opinion of the canonists previously mentioned is thus rendered very doubtful. In this case the fourth section of canon six becomes applicable, and so the pre-Code interpretation should be followed in any case. "Correctio jurium, cum sit odiosa, non sit praesumenda." [50] There is no taxative compilation of the matters concerning which the commissions should be consulted, the decision being left to the prudent judgment of the Bishop. A directive norm may be found in the enumeration already mentioned when dealing with the competence of the two commissions.

3.—*Duration of Office*

The tenure of office for the members of the commissions has been definitely limited by the Code [51] to six years. This is a drastic

---

[47] *Summa Juris Canonici*, II, 394.
[48] *Commentarium*, III, 295.
[49] *Hom. and Past. Review*, XXVIII, (1927), 289.
[50] Maroto, *Instutiones Juris Canonici*, p. 160.
[51] Canon 1359 §3.

change from previous legislation, according to which such appointments were permanent. The Bishop may reappoint the deputies, however, at the expiration of their term in office, if he deems it expedient to do so. A grave cause is required for their removal previous to the conclusion of the six year term. The observations heretofore made concerning the removal of officials in general are applicable also to the members of the commissions. The opinion has been advanced that the Bishop may impose the obligation of secrecy upon the deputies under penalty of removal. A refusal on the part of a member of one of the commissions to accede to such a just request on the part of the Bishop would imply that he considered it proper to divulge the matter under consideration. This would seem to constitute a sufficient cause for his removal.[52]

[52] Il Monitore Ecclesiastico, X, 375.

BIBLIOGRAPHY

SOURCES

Acta Apostolicae Sedis (AAS), Romae, 1909-
Acta Ecclesiae Mediolanensis a Sancto Carolo condita, 2 vols., Lyons, 1682.
Acta Sanctae Sedis (ASS), 41 vols., Romae, 1865-1908.
Acta et Decreta Concilii Plenarii Baltimorensis III, Baltimore, 1886.
Acta et Decreta Conciliorum Recentiorum (Collectio Lacensis), 7 vols., Friburgi Brisgoviae.
Baluzius, Stephanus, *Nova Collectio Conciliorum*, 2 vols., Paris, 1683.
Bollandus, Joannes, *Acta Sanctorum*, Vol. II, Paris.
Bullarum Diplomatum et Privilegiorum Sanctorum Romanorum Pontificum, 25 vols., Augustae Taurinorum, 1857-72.
Canones et Decreta Concilii Tridentini, 19 ed., Taurini, 1913.
Codex Juris Canconici Pii X Pontificis Maximi jussu digestus Benedicti Papae XV autoritate promulgatus, Romae, 1918.
Codicis Juris Canonici Fontes, 4 vols., Romae, 1923-26.
Collectanea in usum Sacrae Congregationis Episcoporum et Regularium, Romae, 1885.
Corpus Juris Canonici, editio Lipsiensis secunda, 2 vols., Lipsiae, 1929.
Corpus Juris Civilis, 3 vols., Berolini, 1928-29.
Harduin, Joannes, *Conciliorum Collectio Regia Maxima*, 12 vols., Paris, 1715.
Labbaeus, Phil., *Sacrorum Conciliorum Nova et Amplissima Collectio*, 29 vols., Florence, 1759.
Mansi, Joannes, *Sacrorum Conciliorum Nova et Amplissima Collectio*, 51 vols., Paris, 1901-27.
Pallottini, Salvatoris, *Collectio Omnium Conclusionum et Resolutionum quae in causis propositis apud S. Cong. Cardinalium, S. Concilii Tridentini Interpretum progierunt ab anno 1564 ad annum 1860*, 17 vols., Romae, 1868-93.
Thesaurus Resolutionum Sacrae Congregationis Concilii, 167 vols., Romae, 1718-1908.
Zamboni, P., *Collectio Declarationum Sacrae Congregationis Cardinalium Sacrae Concilii Tridentini Interpretum*, 4 vols., Attrebati, 1860.

REFERENCE WORKS

Allies, T. W., *The Monastic Life*, London, 1896.
Alzog, John, *Universal Church History*, 3 vols. Cincinnati, 1874.
Ayrinhac, H. A., *General Legislation in the New Code of Canon Law*, New York, 1930.
[Bachofen], Charles Augustine, *A Commentary on the New Code of Canon Law*, 8 vols., St. Louis, 1921-24.
[Bachofen], Charles Augustine, *Summa Juris Publici Ecclesiastici*, Rome, 1910.
Badii, Caesar, *Institutiones Juris Canonici*, 3ed., 2 vol., Florence, 1922.
Barbosa, Aug., *De Officio et Potestate Episcopi*, 2 vols., Lyons, 1656.
Barbosa, Aug., *Tractatus de Canonicis et Dignitatibus*, Lyons, 1679.
Barbosa, Aug., *Sacros Concilii Tridentini Canones et Decreta cum citationibus necnon remissionibus*, Romae, 1621.
Bargilliat, M., *Praelectiones Juris Canonici*, 37ed., 2 vols., Paris, 1923.
Bargilliat, M., *Monita et Decreta de Institutione Clericorum in Seminariis Episcopalibus*, Paris, 1908.

Bastnagel, C., *The Appointment of Parochial Adjutants and Assistants*, Washington, 1930.
Benedict XIV, *De Synodo Diocesana*, 2 vols., Parma, 1764.
Benedict XIV, *Institutiones Ecclestiasticae*, 3 vols., Louvain, 1762.
Bingham, J., *Antiquities of the Christian Church*, 6 vols., London, 1856.
Birkhaeuser, J., *History of the Church*, New York, 1888.
Blat, A., *Commentarium Textus Codicis Juris Canonici*, 6 vols., Rome, 1921-27.
Bonal, A., *Institutiones Canonici ad usum Seminariorum*, 4ed., 2 vols., Paris, 1898.
Bouix, D., *Tractatus de Capitulis*, Paris, 1882.
Bouix, D., *Tractatus de Episcopo*, 2ed., 2 vols., Paris, 1873.
Brueck, Heinrich, *History of the Catholic Church*, 2 vols., New York, 1885.
Buckley, Theodore, *Canons and Decrees of the Council of Trent*, London, 1851.
Catholic Encyclopedia, The, 17 vols., New York, 1907-22.
Cappello, Felix, *Summa Juris Publici Ecclesiastici*, Rome, 1923.
Cappello, Felix, *Summa Juris Canonici in usum scholarum concinnata*, 2 vols., Rome, 1928-30.
Cappello, Felix, *Tractatus Canonico—Moralis de Sacramentis*, 3 vols., Rome, 1921-29.
Cavagnis, F., *Institutiones Juris Publici Ecclesiastici*, 3 vols., Rome, 1883.
Cecconi, Leonardo, *Institutizione dei Seminari Vescovili*, Rome, 1776.
Chelodi, Joannes, *Jus de Personis*, 2ed., Tridenti, 1927.
Chelodi, *Jus Poenale, et Ordo Procedendi in Judiciis Ecclesiasticis juxta Codicem Juris Canonici*, Tridenti, 1925.
Cocchi, Guidus, *Commentarium in Codicem Juris Canonici ad usum Scholarum*, 3ed., 8 vols., Taurinorum Augustae, 1925-27.
Corradus, Pyrrhus, *Praxis Beneficiaria*, Venice, 1736.
D'Angelo, S., *La Curia Dioecesana a norma del Codice di Diritto Canonico*, Giarre, 2 vols., 1923-28.
De Ligouri, A. M., *Oeuvres Completes du Bienhereux*, Vol. XII, 1835.
De Meester, R., *Institutiones Juris Canonici*, 2 vols., Paris, 1853.
De Meester, A., *Juris Canonici et Juris Canonico-Civilis Compendium*, 3 vols., Brugis, 1921-28.
Dictionnaire D'Archeologie Chrétienne et de Liturgie, 18 vols., Paris, 1924-30.
Drane, Augusta, *Christian Schools and Scholars*, London, 1881.
Dubourguier, l'Abbé, *Grandes Ecoles et Gens d'Eglise*, Amiens, 1904.
Duchesne, L., *Liber Pontificalis*, 2 vols., Paris, 1886.
Duchesne, L., *The Early History of the Christian Church*, New York, 1909.
Encyclopedia of Religion and Ethics, 12 vols., New York, 1908-22.
Encyclopédie de la Théologie Catholique, 26 vols., Paris, 1858-68.
Encyclopadisches Handbuch der Pedagogik, 10 vols., Langensalzer, 1903-10.
Fanfani, L., *De Jure Parochorum ad Norman Codicis Juris Canonici*, Taurini-Romae, 1924.
Ferraris, L., *Bibliotheca Canonica, Juridica, Moralis, Theologica, necnon, Ascetica, Polemica, Rubristica et Historica*, 9 vols., Romae, 1885-99.
Ferry W., *Stole Fees*, Washington, 1930.
Gibbons, James Cardinal, *The Ambassador of Christ*, Baltimore, 1896.
Gillet, P., *La, Personallité Juridique en Droit Ecclésiastique*, Malines, 1927.
Giraldi U., *Expositio Juris Pontificii*, 2 vols., Romae, 1829.
Giussano, Jean, *Life of St. Charles Borromeo*, London, 1884.
Hedley, J. C., *Lex Levitarum*, New York, 1905.
Hefele, C., *Conciliengeschichte*, 2 ed., 9 vols., Friedburg, 1873-90.
Hinschius, P., *System des Katholischen Kirchenrechts*, 4 vols., Berlin, 1869-88.
Icard, *Traditions de la Compagnie des Prêtres de St. Sulpice*, Paris, 1886.
Jewish Encyclopedia, The, 12 vols., New York, 1906.
Joly, Claude. *Traitte Historique des Ecoles Episcopales et Ecclésiastiques*, Paris, 1678.

Koch, E. J., *Manual of Apologetics*, New York, 1915.
Lexikon der Pedagogik, 5 vols., Friedburg, 1913-17.
Limmer, R., *Bildungszustande und Bildungsideen des XIII Jahrhunderts*, Munich, 1928.
Lowrie, *The Church and its Organizations*, New York, 1904.
Lucidi, Angelo, *De Visitatione Sacrorum Liminum*, 2 vols., Taurini, 1865.
Mabillon, Joannis, *Praefationes in Acta Sanctorum Ordinis Sancti Benedicti conjunctim editae*, Venice, 1740.
Mabillon, Joannis, *Acta Sanctorum Ordinis Sancti Benedicti in Classes saeculorum distributa*, 9 vols., Venice, 1783.
Makèe, Ch., *Institutiones Juris Ecclesiastici*, 3 vols., Romae, 1897.
Mâitre, P., *Les Ecoles Episcopales et Monastiques en Occident avant les Universités*, 2ed., Paris, 1924.
Marcault, O., *Essai Historique sur l'Education des Clercs*, Paris, 1904.
Maroto, P., *Institutiones Juris Canonici*, 2 vols., Romae, 1919-21.
Melo, A., *De Exemptione Regularium*, Washington, 1921.
McCormick, P. J., *History of Education*, Washington, 1915.
Mercati, Angelo, *Raccolta di Concordati su Materie Ecclesiastiche tra la Santa Sede e le Autorita Civile*, Rome, 1919.
Micheletti, A., *Jus Pianum*, Augustae Taurinorum, 1914.
Mommsen, and Marquardt, *Manuel des Antiquités Romaines*, Vol. XVI, Paris, 1894.
Micheletti, A., *De Regimine Ecclesiastico Religiosorum necnon Seminariorum*, Rome, 1909.
Micheletti, A., *De Ratione Studiorum in Sacris Seminariis*, Rome, 1908.
Micheletti, A., *Consitutiones Seminariorum Clericalium*, Turin, 1919.
Migne, J. P., *Patrologiae Latinae Cursus Completus*, 221 vols., Paris, 1844-55.
Migne, J. P., *Patrologiae Graecae Cursus Completus*, 161 vols., Paris, 1857-87.
Murray, Craigie, Bradley, *New English Dictionary*, 18 vols., Oxford, 1888.
Nussi, V., *Conventiones de Rebus Ecclesiasticis inter Sanctam Sedem et Potestatem Civilem*, Morguntiae, 1870.
Ojetti, B., *Synopsis Rerum Moralium et Juris Pontificii*, Romae, 1909.
Pallavicino, Sforza, *Istoria del Concilio di Trento*, 4 vols., Rome, 1933.
Paulsen, F., *Pedagogik*, Berlin 1911.
Pelella, J., *Canones et Decreta Concilli Tridentini ex editione Romana repetiti*, Naples, 1859.
Pignatelli, J., *Consultationes Canonicae*, 9 vols., Coloniae Allobrogum, 1700.
Pouan, B., *Dissertatio Historico-Canonica de Seminario Clericorum*, Louvain, 1874.
Probst, F., *Kirchliche Disciplin in den drei ersten Christlichen Jahrhunderten*, Tubingen, 1873.
Probst, F., *Lehre und Gebet in den drei ersten Christlichen Jahrhunderten*, Tubingen, 1871.
Prümmer, D., *Manuale Juris Canonici*, 3 ed., Freigurg, 1922.
Rashdall, *Universities of Europe in the Middle Ages*, Oxford, 1895.
Reiffenstuel, A., *Jus Canonicum Universum*, 4 vols., Romae, 1833.
Robert, G., *Les Ecoles et l'Enseignement dans la Moitié du Siècle XII*, Paris,
Robert, G., *Les Ecoles et l'Enseignement dans la Moitié du Siecle XII*, Paris, 1909.
Sandys, J., *Companion to Latin Studies*, Cambridge, Mass., 1929.
Schaff, *History of the Christian Church*, New York, 1895.
Schmalzgrueber, F., *Jus Ecclesiasticum Universum*, 12 vols., Romae, 1843-45.
Schmidt, K., *Geschichte der Pedagogik*, 3 vols., Cathen, 1873.
Stöckl, A., *Lehrbuch der Geschichte der Pedagogik*, Mainz, 1876.
Smith, J. T., *The Training of a Priest*, New York, 1908.
Stephanus, M., *Commentarium in Novellas*, Florence, 1843.
Tanquerey, A., *Synopsis Thologiae Dogmaticae*, 3 vols., Romae, 1925.
Theiner, Aug., *Histoire des Institutions d'Education Ecclésiastique*, Translated from the German by Jean Cohen, 2 vols., Paris, 1841.

Themistor, Irenee, *L'Instruction et L'Education du Clergé*, Treves, 1884.
Thomassinus, L., *Nova et Vetus Disciplina Ecclesiae*, 10 vols., Moguntiaci, 1787.
Trezzini, *La Legislazione Canonica di Gelasio I*, Locarno, 1911.
Van-Espen, Z., *Jus Ecclesiasticum Universum*, 4 vols., Louvain, 1753.
Van Hove, *De Legibus Ecclesiasticis*, Malines, 1930.
Vecchiotti, S. M., *Institutiones Canonicae ad usum Seminariorum accomadatae*, 19 ed., Augustae Taurinorum, 1886.
Vermeersch, A.-Creusen, J., *Epitome Juris Canonici*, 3 vols., Mechlinae-Romae, 1925-27.
Vromant, G., *De Bonis Ecclesiae Temporalibus*, Louvain, 1927.
Wernz, F. X., *Jus Decretalium*, vol. III, Romae, 1908.
Wernz, F. X., Videl, P., *Jus Canonicum ad Codicis norman exactum*, 3 vols., Romae, 1925-28.
Woywod, S., *A Practical Commentary on the Code of Canon Law*, 2 vols., New York, 1925.
Zallwein, P., *Principia Juris Ecclesiastici*, 4 vols., Augustae, 1763.

PERIODICALS

American Ecclesiastical Review, The, (AER), Philadelphia, 1889-
Analecta Ecclesiastica, Romae, 1893-1911.
Analecta Juris Pontificii, Romae, 1855-68; Parisisiis, 1869-1890.
Ephemerides Theologicae Lovaniensis, Louvain, 1924-
Homiletic and Pastoral Review, The, New York, 1900-
Il Monitore Ecclesiastico, Romae, 1888-
Le Canoniste Contemporain, Paris, 1878-
Jus Pontificium, Romae, 1921-
Nouvelle Revue Théologique (NRT), Tournai, 1869.
Revue des Sciences Ecclésiastiques, Arras, 1860-1906.
Periodica de re canonica et morali utili praesertim Religiosis et missionariis, Bruges, 1905-

UNIVERSITAS CATHOLICA AMERICAE

WASHINGTON, D. C.

FACULTAS IURIS CANONICI

1931

No. 67

DEUS LUX MEA

TITULI

QUOS

AD DOCTORATUS GRADUM

IN

JURE CANONICO

Apud Universitatem Catholicam Americae

CONSEQUENDUM

PUBLICE PROPUGNAVIT

JOSEPHUS G. COX

SACERDOS ARCHIDIOECESIS PHILADELPHIENSIS

JURIS CANONICI LICENTIATUS

HORA IX AM DIE XXV MAII MCMXXXI

TITULI

DE JURE CANONICO

I.	De Dissertatione.	
II.	De Historia Juris Canonici.	
III.	Canones 1-7	De Ambitu Codicis.
IV.	Canones 8-24	De Legibus Ecclesiasticis.
V.	Canones 25-30	De Consuetudine.
VI.	Canones 31-35	De Temporis Supputatione.
VII.	Canones 36-62	De Rescriptis.
VIII.	Canones 63-79	De Privilegiis.
IX.	Canones 80-86	De Dispensationibus.
X.	Canones 87-107	Generales Notiones de Personis.
XI.	Canones 111-117	De Clericorum Adscriptione Alicui Dioecesi.
XII.	Canones 118-123	De Juribus et Privilegiis Clericorum.
XIII.	Canones 124-144	De Obligationibus Clericorum.
XIV.	Canones 145-195	De Officiis Ecclesiasticis.
XV.	Canones 196-210	De Potestate Ordinaria et Delegata.
XVI.	Canones 211-214	De Reductione Clericorum ad Statum Laicalem.
XVII.	Canones 487-498	De Notione Religionis, et de Erectione et Suppressione Religionis, Provinciae, Domus.
XVIII.	Canones 499-537	De Religionum Regimine.
XIX.	Canones 538-586	De Admissione in Religionem.
XX.	Canones 587-591	De Ratione Studiorum in Religionibus Clericalibus.
XXI.	Canones 592-631	De Obligationibus et Privilegiis Religiosorum.
XXII.	Canones 632-672	De Transitu ad Aliam Religionem, de Egressu e Religione, et de Dimissione Religiosorum.
XXIII.	Canones 673-681	De Societatibus sive Virorum sive Mulierum in Communi Viventium sine Votis.
XXIV.	Canones 1012-1018	De Matrimonio in Genere.
XXV.	Canones 1019-1034	De Iis Quae Matrimonii Celebrationi Praemitti Debent.
XXVI.	Canones 1035-1057	De Impedimentis in Genere.
XXVII.	Canones 1058-1066	De Impedimentis Impedientibus.
XXVIII.	Canones 1067-1080	De Impedimentis Dirimentibus.
XXIX.	Canones 1081-1093	De Consensu Matrimoniale.

XXX.	Canones 1552-1568	De Notione Judicii et de Foro Competenti.
XXXI.	Canones 1569-1607	De Variis Tribunalium Gradibus et Speciebus.
XXXII.	Canones 1608-1645	De Disciplina in Tribunalibus Servanda.
XXXIII.	Canones 1646-1666	De Partibus in Causa.
XXXIV.	Canones 1667-1705	De Actionibus et Exceptionibus.
XXXV.	Canones 1706-1725	De Causae Introductione.
XXXVI.	Canones 1726-1746	De Litis Contestatione, de Litis Instantia, et de Interrogationibus Partibus in Judicio Faciendis.
XXXVII.	Canones 1747-1836	De Probationibus.
XXXVIII.	Canones 1837-1857	De Causis Incidentibus.
XXXIX.	Canones 2195-2198	De Natura Delicti Ejusque Divisione.
XL.	Canones 2199-2211	De Imputabilitate Delicti, de Causis Illam Aggravantibus vel Minuentibus, et de Juridicis Delicti Effectibus.
XLI.	Canones 2212-2213	De Conatu Delicti.
XLII.	Canones 2214-2240	De Poenis in Genere.
XLIII.	Canones 2241-2285	De Poenis Medicinalibus seu de Censuris.
XLIV.	Canones 2286-2305	De Poenis Vindicativis.
XLV.	Canones 2306-2313	De Remediis Poenalibus et Poenitentiis.

DE JURE ROMANO

XLVI. The Periods of Roman Law.
XLVII. The Sources of Roman Law.
XLVIII. Personality.
XLIX. Slavery.
L. Citizenship.
LI. Patria Potestas.
LII. Personae in Manu.
LIII. Personae in Mancipio.
LIV. Tutela et Cura.
LV. Ownership.
LVI. De Obligationibus in Genere.
LVII. De Obligationibus Extra-Contractualibus.
LVIII. Furtum.
LIX. Damnum Injuria Datum.
LX. Injuria.

Vidit Facultas:

VALENTINUS T. SCHAAF, O.F.M., J.C.D., Decanus Substitutus.

LUDOVICUS H. MOTRY, S.T.D., J.C.D.

FRANCISCUS J. LARDONE, S.T.D., J.U.D.

Vidit Rector Magnificus Universitatis:

JACOBUS HUGO RYAN, Ph.D., S.T.D.

BIOGRAPHICAL NOTE

Joseph G. Cox was born in Philadelphia, Pa., January 17, 1903. He attended St. Joseph's parochial school and the Cathedral School, and then entered the Roman Catholic High School, from which he graduated in 1921. In September of the same year he entered St. Charles' Seminary, Overbrook. In 1929 he matriculated at the Catholic University of America. He was ordained to the Priesthood on May 30, 1930, by Rt. Rev. Gerald P. O'Hara, Auxiliary Bishop of Philadelphia.

CATHOLIC UNIVERSITY OF AMERICA

CANON LAW STUDIES

1. FRERIKS REV. CELESTINE A., C.PP.S., J.C.D., Religious Congregations in Their External Relations, 121 pp., 1916.
2. GALLIHER, REV. DANIEL M., O.P., J.C.D., Canonical Elections, 117 pp., 1917.
3. BORKOWSKI, REV. AURELIUS L., O.F.M., J.C.D., De Confraternitatibus Ecclesiasticis, 136 pp., 1918.
4. CASTILLO, REV. CAYO, J.C.D., Disertacion Historico-canonica sobre la Potestad del Cabildo en Sede Vacante o Impedida del Vicario Capitular, 99 pp., 1919 (1918).
5. KUBELBECK, REV. WILLIAM J., S.T.B., J.C.D., The Sacred Penitentiaria and Its Relations to Faculties of Ordinaries and Priests, 129 pp., 1918.
6. PETROVITS, REV. JOSEPH J. C., S.T.D., J.C.D., The New Church Law on Matrimony, X-461 pp., 1919.
7. HICKEY, REV. JOHN J., S.T.B., J.C.D., Irregularities and Simple Impediments in the New Code of Canon Law, 100 pp., 1920.
8. KLEKOTKA, REV. PETER J., S.T.B., J.C.D., Diocesan Consultors, 179 pp., 1920.
9. WANNENMACHER, REV. FRANCIS, J.C.D., The Evidence in Ecclesiastical Procedure Affecting the Marriage Bond, 1920. (Not Printed.)
10. GOLDEN, REV. HENRY FRANCIS, J.C.D., Parochial Benefices in the New Code, IV-119 pp., 1921. (Printed 1925.)
11. KOUDELKA, REV. CHARLES J., J.C.D., Pastors, Their Rights and Duties According to the New Code of Canon Law, 211 pp., 1921.
12. MELO, REV. ANTONIUS, O.F.M., J.C.D., De Exemptione Regularium, X-188 pp., 1921.
13. SCHAAF, REV. VALENTINE THEODORE, O.F.M., S.T.B., J.C.D., The Cloister, X-180 pp., 1921.
14. BURKE, REV. THOMAS JOSEPH, S.T.B., J.C.D., Competence in Ecclesiastical Tribunals, IV-117 pp., 1922.
15. LEECH, REV. GEORGE LEO, J.C.D., A Comparative Study of the Constitution "Apostolicae Sedis" and the "Codex Juris Canonici," 179 pp., 1922.
16. MOTRY, REV. HUBERT LOUIS, S.T.D., J.C.D., Diocesan Faculties According to the Code of Canon Law, II-167 pp., 1922.
17. MURPHY, REV. GEORGE LAWRENCE, J.C.D., Delinquencies and Penalties in the Administration and the Reception of the Sacraments, IV-121 pp., 1923.
18. O'REILLY, REV. JOHN ANTHONY, S.T.B., J.C.D., Ecclesiastical Sepulture in the New Code of Canon Law, II-129 pp., 1923.
19. MICHALICKA, REV. WENCESLAS CYRILL, O.S.B., J.C.D., Judicial Procedure in Dismissal of Clerical Exempt Religious, 107 pp., 1923.

20. DARGIN, REV. EDWARD VINCENT, S.T.B., J.C.D., Reserved Cases According to the Code of Canon Law, IV-103 pp., 1924.
21. GODFREY, REV. JOHN A., S.T.B., J.C.D., The Right of Patronage According to the Code of Canon Law, 153 pp., 1924.
22. HAGEDORN, REV. FRANCIS EDWARD, J.C.D., General Legislation on Indulgences, II-154 pp., 1924.
23. KING, REV. JAMES IGNATIUS, J.C.D., The Administration of the Sacraments to Dying Non-Catholics, V-141 pp., 1924.
24. WINSLOW, REV. FRANCIS JOSEPH, A.F.M., J.C.D., Vicars and Prefects Apostolic, IV-149 pp., 1924.
25. CORREA, REV. JOSE SERVELION, S.T.L., J.C.D., La Potestad Legislativa de la Iglesia Catolica, IV-127 pp., 1925.
26. DUGAN, REV. HENRY FRANCIS, M.A., J.C.D., The Judiciary Department of the Diocesan Curia, 87 pp., 1925.
27. KELLER, REV. CHARLES FREDERICK, S.T.B., J.C.D., Mass Stipends, 167 pp., 1925.
28. PASCHANG, REV. JOHN LINUS, J.C.D., The Sacramentals According to the Code of Canon Law, 129 pp., 1925.
29. PIONTEK, REV. CYRILLUS, O.F.M., S.T.B., J.C.D., De Indulto Exclaustrationis necnon Saecularizationis, XIII-289 pp., 1925.
30. KEARNEY, REV. RICHARD JOSEPH, S.T.B., J.C.D., Sponsors at Baptism According to the Code of Canon Law, IV-127 pp., 1925.
31. BARTLETT, REV. CHESTER JOSEPH, A.M., LL.B., J.C.D., The Tenure of Parochial Property in the United States of America, V-108 pp., 1926.
32. KILKER, REV. ADRIAN JEROME, J.C.D., Extreme Unction, V-425 pp., 1926.
33. MCCORMICK, REV. ROBERT EMMET, J.C.D., Confessors of Religious, VIII-266 pp., 1926.
34. MILLER, REV. NEWTON THOMAS, J.C.D., Founded Masses According to the Code of Canon Law, VII-93 pp., 1926.
35. ROELKER, REV. EDWARD G., S.T.D., J.C.D., Principles of Privilege According to the Code of Canon Law, XI-166 pp., 1926.
36. BAKALARCZYK, REV. RICHARDUS, M.I.C., J.U.D., De Novitiatu, VIII-208 pp., 1927.
37. PIZZUTI, REV. LAWRENCE, O.F.M., J.U.L., De Parochis Religiosis, 1927. (Not Printed.)
38. BLILEY, REV. NICHOLAS MARTIN, O.S.B., J.C.D., Altars According to the Code of Canon Law, XIX-132 pp., 1927.
39. BROWN, BRENDAN FRANCIS, A.B., LL.M., J.U.D., The Canonical Juristic Personality with Special Reference to its Status in the United States of America, V-212 pp., 1927.
40. CAVANAUGH, REV. WILLIAM THOMAS, C.P., J.U.D., The Reservation of the Blessed Sacrament, VIII-101 pp., 1927.
41. DOHENY, REV. WILLIAM J., C.S.C., A.B., J.U.D., Church Property: Modes of Acquisition, X-118 pp., 1927.
42. FELDHAUS, REV. ALOYSIUS H., C.PP.S., J.C.D., Oratories, IX-141 pp., 1927.
43. KELLY, REV. JAMES PATRICK, A.B., J.C.D., The Jurisdiction of the Simple Confessor, X-208 pp., 1927.
44. NEUBERGER, REV. NICHOLAS J., J.C.D., Canon 6 or the Relation of the Codex Juris Canonici to the Preceding Legislation, V-95 pp., 1927.

45. O'Keeffe, Rev. Gerald Michael, J.C.D., Matrimonial Dispensations, Powers of Bishops, Priests, and Confessors, VIII-232 pp., 1927.
46. Quigley, Rev. Joseph, A.M., A.B., J.C.D., Condemmed Societies, 139 pp. 1927.
47. Zaplotnik, Rev. Ioannes Leo, J.C.D., De Vicariis Foraneis, X-142 1927.
48. Duskie, Rev. John Aloysius, A.B., J.C.D., The Canonical Status of the Orientals in the United States, VIII-196 pp., 1928.
49. Hyland, Rev. Francis Edward, J.C.D., Excommunication, Its Nature, Historical Development and Effects, VIII-181 pp., 1928.
50. Reinmann, Rev. Gerald Joseph, O.M.C., J.C.D., The Third Order Secular of Saint Francis, 201 pp., 1928.
51. Schenk, Rev. Francis J., J.C.D., The Matrimonial Impediments of Mixed Religion and Disparity of Cult. XVI-318 pp., 1929.
52. Coady, Rev. John Joseph, S.T.D., J.U.D., A.M., The Appointment of Pastors, VIII-150 pp., 1929.
53. Kay, Rev. Thomas Henry, J.C.D., Competence in Matrimonial Procedure, VIII-164 pp., 1929.
54. Turner, Rev. Sidney Joseph, C.P., J.U.D., The Vow of Poverty, XLIX-217 pp., 1929.
55. Kearney, Rev. Raymond A., A.B., S.T.D., J.C.D., The Principles of Delegation, VII-149 pp., 1929.
56. Conran, Rev. Edward James, A.B., J.C.L., The Interdict, 1930.
57. O'Neill, Rev. William H., J.C.L., Papal Rescripts of Favor, 1930.
58. Bastnagel, Rev. Clement Vincent, J.U.L., The Appointment of Parochial Adjutants and Assistants, 1930.
59. Ferry, Rev. William A., A.B., J.C.L., Stole Fees, 1930.
60. Costello, Rev. John Michael, A.B., J.C.L., Domicile and Quasi-Domicile, 1930.
61. Kremer, Rev. Michael Nicholas, A.B., S.T.B., J.C.L., Church Support in the United States, 1930.
62. Angulo, Rev. Luis Martinez, C.M., J.C.L., Legislacion de la Iglesia Catolica sobre la intencion en la applicacion de la Misa, 1931.
63. Frey, Rev. Wolfgang N., O.S.B., A.B., J.C.L., The Act of Religious Profession, 1931.
64. Roberts, Rev. James B., A.B., J.C.L., The Banns of Marriage, 1931.
65. Ryder, Rev. Raymond A., A.B., J.C.L., Simony, 1931.
66. Campagna, Rev. Michael A., Ph.B., J.U.L., Il Vicario Generale del Vescovo, 1931.
67. Cox, Rev. Joseph G., A.B., J.C.L., The Administration of Seminaries, 1931.
68. Gregory, Rev. Donald J., S.T.B., J.U.L., The Pauline Privilege, 1931.
69. Donohue, Rev. John F., M.A., J.C.L., The Impediment of Crime, 1931.
70. Dooly, Rev. Eugene A., O.M.I., J.C.L., Church Law on Sacred Relics, 1931

www.ingramcontent.com/pod-product-compliance
Lightning Source LLC
LaVergne TN
LVHW050205080826
844660LV00012B/360

9780813222561